Ökonomische Analyse des Rechts | Economic Analysis of Law

Die ökonomische Analyse des Rechts untersucht Rechtsnormen auf ihre gesellschaftlichen Folgewirkungen und bedient sich dabei des methodischen Instrumentariums der Wirtschaftswissenschaften. Sie ist ein interdisziplinäres Forschungsgebiet, in dem sowohl Rechtswissenschaftler als auch Wirtschaftswissenschaftler tätig sind und das zu wesentlichen neuen Erkenntnissen über Funktion und Wirkungen von Rechtsnormen geführt hat. Die Schriftenreihe enthält Monographien zu verschiedenen Rechtsgebieten und Rechtsentwicklungen.
Die Buchreihe wird als Fortsetzung der Reihe „Ökonomische Analyse des Rechts“ geführt.

The economic analysis of law examines legal norms drawing on the economic approach. The analysis does not only include the consequences of legal norms but also the determinants of their emergence. It is an interdisciplinary research program in which both lawyers as well as economists are active. Over the last half century, some of its contributions have lead to important insights regarding the emergence, the functioning, as well as the effects of legal norms. This series is a forum for contributions to the economic analysis of law broadly conceived.
The book series is a continuation of the series Economic Analysis of Law.

More information about this series at http://www.springer.com/series/16196

Goran Dominioni

Biased Trials

Insights from Behavioral Law and Economics

Springer Gabler

Goran Dominioni
Washington, D.C., USA

Dissertation Bologna University, Erasmus University Rotterdam, Hamburg University, 2018

ISSN 2524-7360 ISSN 2524-7379 (electronic)
Ökonomische Analyse des Rechts | Economic Analysis of Law
ISBN 978-3-658-30079-1 ISBN 978-3-658-30080-7 (eBook)
https://doi.org/10.1007/978-3-658-30080-7

This Springer Gabler imprint is published by the registered company Springer Fachmedien Wiesbaden GmbH part of Springer Nature.
The registered company address is: Abraham-Lincoln-Str. 46, 65189 Wiesbaden, Germany

To mom and dad

Table of Contents

List of Abbreviations

EU:	European Union
FAE:	Fundamental Attribution Error
fMRI:	Functional Magnetic Resonance Imaging
IAT:	Implicit Association Test
IRBs:	Implicit Racial Biases
JDM:	Judgment and Decision-Making
R.D.:	Royal Decree
SES:	Socioeconomic Status
WTA:	Willingness to Accept
WTP:	Willingness to Pay

List of Tables and Figures

1 The Behavioral Economics of Accuracy and Discrimination at Trial: An Introduction

1.1 Aim and Scope

A fundamental issue underlying the regulation of human societies via law is whether and to what extent we are able to accurately describe and predict how legal rules affect behavior.[1] When drafting laws, legislators can (and hopefully do) take into account how the law will affect the behavior of the relevant population. In doing so, they may (and, again, hopefully do) consider how individuals called to enforce these laws are likely to perform. Traditional legal scholars often rely on implicit assumptions based on intuitions to study how the law and its enforcement affects behavior.[2] While acting on the basis of intuitions can sometimes lead to desired outcomes, it may also leave several problems unaddressed or lead to undesired consequences. Law and economics represents a major advancement in legal scholarship towards the explicitation of the behavioral assumptions underlying law-making and policymaking. Based on rational choice theory, law and economics has powerfully improved our ability to accurately predict the effects of legal rules on human conduct. Also, the explicitation of the assumptions underlying rational choice theory has allowed their rigorous testing which, in turn, has led to a more refined understanding of how law affects human behavior. A main result of this scientific endeavour in the legal sphere is a strand of legal literature that builds on both economics and psychology, and is referred to as behavioral law and economics.[3] The main aim of this book is to study the interplay of accuracy and the behavioral economics of evidence law in tort trials.

---

1 Donald C. Langevoort, 1998. Behavioral Theories of Judgment and Decision Making in Legal Scholarship: A Literature Review, 51 VAND. L. REV. 1499.

2 Avishalom Tor, 2008. The Methodology of the Behavioral Analysis of Law. 4 HAIFA LAW REVIEW 239.

3 Christine Jolls, Cass R. Sunstein, and Richard Thaler, 1998. A Behavioral Approach to Law and Economics. 50(5) STAN. L. REV. 1471; Russell B. Korobkin, and Thomas S. Ulen (2000). 88(4) Law and Behavioral Science: Removing the Rationality Assumption from Law and Economics. CALIF. LAW REV 1051.

G. Dominioni, *Biased Trials*, Ökonomische Analyse des Rechts | Economic Analysis of Law, https://doi.org/10.1007/978-3-658-30080-7_1

The interplay between accuracy and behavioral economics is discussed here from three perspectives, each of which refers to one of three related streams of literature. The first issue that is addressed in this book is whether the alleged increased accuracy of behavioral economics vis-à-vis neoclassical economics in describing human behavior can lead to policy-relevant insights. Here accuracy refers to whether our understanding of human behavior improves when insights from neoclassical economics are combined with behavioral ones. While most authors believe that indeed a behavioral approach can lead to a more accurate description of human behavior, the extent to which this increased accuracy can be useful for policymaking is a much more controversial issue.[4] Besides the skepticism of some economically minded scholars and policymakers towards some of the methods adopted in behavioral sciences, a potential limit of behavioral economics to inform policymaking is that it does not provide a unified theory of human decision-making.[5] The primarily inductive method adopted by behavioral studies may lead to results that do not provide clear-cut predictions of how people will behave in a given situation, thus limiting their usefulness for ex-ante regulation.

Throughout this book, I will argue that behavioral insights can be useful for policymaking in the areas of evidence law and tort law, at least in two main ways. First, when we focus on the decision-making of trial participants (judges, witnesses, expert testimonies), behavioral economics allows understanding how different items of information that enter the trial context are likely to affect courts' decisions. Thus, a behavioral approach can unveil hidden patterns in the functioning of tort law systems. These patterns can be fairly clear-cut and thus offer some predictions for policymakers. This is even more so when multiple behavioral phenomena point in the same direction. Second, once discovered, these patterns can be left untouched or (maybe partially), addressed depending on the costs and benefits of doing so in light of the normative criterion/a adopted in the analysis. In this regard, it is often the case that the most effective and efficient policies to address these unwarranted patterns build on behavioral sciences.

4 Michael Faure 2010. Behavioural Accident Law and Economics. 4 J. APPL. ECON 11. Note however, that behavioural insights are already applied to policy, see for instance: Goran Dominioni and Dirk Heine, 2019. Behavioural Economics and Public Support for Carbon Pricing: A Revenue Recycling Scheme to Address the Political Economy of Carbon Taxation, 10(3) EUROPEAN JOURNAL OF RISK REGULATION 554-570.

5 Richard A. Posner, 1998. Rational Choice, Behavioral Economics, and the Law. STAN. L. REV. 1551; Michael Faure, 2010.

Overall, this book highlights that a behavioral approach can contribute to reveal the effects of existing procedural rules and court practices. As such, this type of analysis can complement neoclassical studies in providing guidance to policymakers regarding how to best regulate a particular activity. While most of the issues addressed in this book are relevant for the study of tort law from the perspective of corrective justice and distributive justice, the approach taken here is purely welfarist.

The second perspective from which this book addresses the interplay between accuracy and behavioral law and economics is captured in the following questions: does behavioral economics suggests that we should trust courts to make accurate decisions at trial? If yes, under what circumstances? Contrary to above, accuracy refers here to the correspondence of courts' decision-making with the empirical reality of the facts under scrutiny at trial, i.e., what in legal jargon is usually referred to as absence of errors in fact. As I will discuss in the following pages, accuracy in adjudication is commonly valued in tort law scholarship, as it is related to justice and welfare maximization. This book highlights that indeed findings in behavioral sciences cast doubts on courts' ability to make accurate decisions. Yet, the analysis also reveals that the link between behavioral findings and accuracy at trial is often more complex than generally assumed by legal scholars. Thus, I call for more caution when applying behavioral findings to the study of law and policymaking.

Lastly, the third question addressed in this book is: does a behavioral approach to law make accuracy (i.e. correct decisions) a less compelling aim of adjudication? In neoclassical law and economics it is often argued that in a world in which increasing accuracy of adjudication is costless, social welfare maximization can be reached via the pursue of accuracy at trial.[6] Throughout the book I will show that, contrary to this conventional wisdom, a more accurate decision can sometimes be detrimental to social welfare maximization regardless of the procedural costs of making the decision more accurate.

Notice that, in this book, these three perspecitves on the relationship between accuracy at trial and behavioral law and economics are analyzed neither singularly nor in their whole, but by means of Chapters that address a particular topic in the

---

6 Louis Kaplow, 2015. Information and the Aim of Adjudication: Truth or Consequences. 67 STAN. L. REV. 1303.

behavioral analysis of evidence law in tort trials. As such, each Chapter may provide an answer to a question that is only partially overlapping to the one discussed above. It is only when the analysis is seen in its entirety that an answer to the three main questions arises. This, more comprehensive, analysis is offered in the last Chapter of this book.

A latent theme that permeates a large part of this book - circumscribing its scope - is the behavioral economics of ingroup-outgroup biases. Psychologists have long shown that human judgment and decision-making is often influenced by whether the information processed by our mind relates to someone that we perceive as belonging to our social group (being it gender, race, ethnicity, socioeconomic status, etc.) or to another social group. These biases are often related to the reality that individuals experience (directly or indirectly, e.g. via the media) and as such, this theme is strongly linked to the accuracy of judgment, here in a considered from a statistical perspective.

From a legal perspective, the analysis is confined to European and US tort trials. Existing literature on the behavioral economics of evidence law in tort trials is mainly concerned with US law. This book aims to broaden the scope of this inquiry by focusing on European legal systems. The parallel with US law creates synergies in linking the present findings with those of the existent literature.

1.2 Methodology

From a methodological standpoint this book takes a multifold approach. Concerning the legal analysis, I adopt a comparative methodology when this approach is instrumental to answer the specific questions addressed in a Chapter. Chapter 2 makes a comparison between Italian and US law as it addresses the question of whether country differences in the regulation of character evidence can be justified in light of the employment of juries vis-à-vis judges in adjudication. Chapter 4 broadens the scope to encompass an analysis of English, French, Italian, and US law as it aims analyze how these different jurisdictions deal with the use of gender and race-based statistical tables to award damages at trial. In other Chapters, a thorough comparative analysis is less relevant for the research question addressed and, therefore, I make only sporadic references to rules or practices adopted in one or more legal system. In this regard, in Chapter 3, the legal analysis is concerned with whether and how implicit racial biases can affect tort trial outcomes in several European countries, but without the aim of making a comparison between the situation prevailing in different jurisdictions.

The book adopts a multifold approach also concerning the behavioral law and economics side of the analysis. The starting point of each topic analyzed is the neoclassical economic approach to the issue. Subsequently, I expand the analysis to take into account insights from psychology and behavioral economics. Generally, this expansion can take a theoretical or an empirical approach. The analysis provided in this book takes both forms.

Following a well-established methodology, the theoretical Chapters build on existing studies in the abovementioned disciplines and draw parallels between the judgments and decisions made by subjects in experimental settings and evaluations that individuals involved in tort trials (e.g. judges, experts, policemen) perform on a regular basis. In this connection, theoretical research in behavioral law and economics can take two different approaches, either consider what are the consequences of a particular behavioral phenomenon for a branch of the law or, alternatively, analyze a particular legal issue by drawing on multiple behavioral findings.[7] Both approaches are embraced in different Chapters of this book.

An empirical approach is taken in Chapter 3. In the plethora of possible empirical methods used in behavioral law and economics,[8] I carry out a quasi-experimental vignette study. In vignette studies, subjects read a hypothetical scenario and are requested to answer one or more questions related to it. In a fully experimental between-subjects study participants are randomly assigned to different scenarios, so that differences in responses can be linked to the variations in vignettes. In a quasi-experimental design, subjects are not randomly assigned to different conditions. In this case, differences between conditions can be traced back to either subjects characteristics or differences in scenarios. Since the aim of my study is to test whether individuals with different degrees of expertise in adjudication are differently prone to commit a cognitive error in trial settings, the adoption of a quasi-experimental design is an appropriate methodological choice.

---

7 Avishalom Tor (2008).

8 Christoph Engel, 2013. Behavioral Law and Economics: Empirical Methods, MPI COLLECTIVE GOODS PREPRINT, No. 2013/1.

1.2 Scientific and Societal Relevance

From a scientific perspective, each Chapter contributes to a particular strand of literature. Generally, the fields of research to which this study contributes are tort law, evidence law, comparative law, judicial decision-making, and behavioral law and economics. Besides contributing to specific strands of literature, the book generally highlights that relying on neoclassical economics provides only a limited picture of the functioning of tort law systems. In this regard, a major contribution of law and economics to the study of tort law is its focus on the incentives that different rules, standards, and court practices provide to potential tortfeasors and victims.[9] For instance, neoclassical economics provides useful insights on which of two liability regimes (e.g. negligence vs. strict liability) provides stronger incentives to tortfeasors and victims to invest in precautionary measures.[10] The power of law and economics, however, goes even further than this, as it allows assessing the performance of different rules, standards, and practices to achieve social welfare maximization. This, in turn, can provide insightful perspectives for welfare-based policymaking.[11]

Yet, a necessary (and obvious) limit of law and economics is that economic models can capture only a part of reality. For this reason, developments in the literature show that sometimes results that were once well established, might turn out to be weaker when additional factors are taken into account.[12] In this connection, to the extent that policy makers choose to pursue social welfare maximization as the normative aim, the policy recommendation to be followed may change.

Traditionally, the increase in analytical complexity of the functioning of tort law systems was achieved by considering for instance, different types of risk preferences or by adding institutional details previously ignored.[13] Behavioral law and economics could be seen as a specific type of this developments, which is characterized by complementing or substituting rational choice theory with other models of decision-making borrowed from psychology and behavioral economics. As I

---

9 Steven Shavell, 2009. Economic Analysis of Accident Law. HARVARD UNIVERSITY PRESS.

10 Steven Shavell, 1980. Strict liability Versus Negligence. 9(1) J. LEGAL STUD. 1.

11 See, for instance: Michael Faure, 2015. Private Liability and Critical Infrastructure. 6(2) EUROPEAN JOURNAL OF RISK REGULATION, 229.

12 See, for instance the literature discussed below.

13 See, generally: Michael Faure, 2009. Tort Law and Economics (Vol. 1). EDWARD ELGAR PUBLISHING.

will argue below, the expansion of the analysis to alternative models of decision-making can sometimes highlight that the incentives set by rules, standards, and practices might be different from those resulting from a rational choice analysis. As a consequence, the welfare effects of these legal instruments and practices can be shown to be different from the one previously thought.

To the extent that these alternative models of decision-making capture systematic trends in the way individuals form their judgment and behave, policymaking based solely on rational choice theory may lead to states of the world in which social welfare is lower than if behavioral insights were taken into account. There is an overwhelming amount of evidence that derives from studies in psychology and behavioral economics showing that rational choice theory fails to predict human judgment and decision-making in a wide variety of settings.[14] This evidence provides strong indication that even if a system was shaped to accommodate recommendations that derive from taking an economic approach to study law, there are good reasons to believe that this system would not maximize social welfare. This can happen, for instance, in contexts in which an analysis based on rational choice theory suggests that social welfare is higher if rule A is implemented compared to rule B, but the reverse is true when behavioral insights are taken into account. Behavioral law and economics is therefore a useful complement to more traditional rational choice-based welfare analyses.

Its usefulness is even more manifest if one considers that sometimes the best policy response to decision-making that does not conform to rational choice theory is not to change the rule from A to B, but to combine rule A with another rule. Imagine, for instance, that if rule C complements rule A, social welfare is higher than under rule B and rule B+C. In this case, if A, B, and C are the full set of rules available, A+C is the best policy choice. In this respect, an aspect that makes behavioral law and economics a very useful complement of neoclassical law and economics is that the most efficient and effective policy strategies that aim to address reductions in social welfare due to departures from rational choice are often based on behavioral insights. For example, this is the case of strategies that align the decision-making of the individual with the predictions of rational choice. In this sense, the book highlights the importance of complementing neoclassical economics with a behavioral approach to the study of the functioning of tort law, evidence law, and judicial decision-making.

---

[14] Jolls et al. (1998).

More generally, this book analyzes an issue that is relevant for evaluating the performance of any legal system. Indeed, how accurately we can predict the influence of a legal rule on human behavior is a relevant issue for any policymaker interested in the consequences of her policy choices. This is a non-trivial issue, especially in an era in which behavioral policymaking is becoming more and more pervasive at all levels of governance.[15]

In addition, the accuracy of fact-finding is a major concern of any legal system as it is linked to the achievement of various aims, such as deterrence and justice.[16] Evidentiary rules as well as rules of substantive law are often justified and reformed on the basis of their alleged ability to increase accuracy in adjudication. As it will be discussed extensively in the following pages, the ability of a legal system to reach this goal is not independent from the way in which judges perceive and evaluate items of evidence presented at trial and make decisions on their basis. A behavioral law and economics approach to the study of accuracy at trial can therefore enlighten the strengths and weaknesses of formal and informal rules regulating the trial.

Furthermore, given this widespread belief that accuracy should be a major aim of adjudication, highlighting limits of accuracy for the achievement of other normative values is a non-irrelevant issue.

The societal relevance of this book goes beyond the practical importance of accuracy. A major focus of the present work is on ingroup-outgroup biases, and more specifically on gender and racial issues. These topics are of increasing policy relevance in Europe. Nowadays a large proportion of European residents is of non-European ancestry.[17] This proportion is likely to increase in the near future manly

---

15 See for instance: http://www.worldbank.org/en/programs/gini; https://ec.europa.eu/jrc/en/research/crosscutting-activities/behavioral-insights; World Bank, (2019) State and Trends of Carbon Pricing 2019, State and Trends of Carbon Pricing, WORLD BANK, Washington, DC.

16 Nuno Garoupa and Matteo Rizzolli, 2012. Wrongful Convictions Do Lower Deterrence. 168(2) JITE, 224; Ralph Grunewald, 2013. Comparing Injustices: Truth, Justice, and the System. 77 ALB. L. REV. 1139.

17 In 2009, Germany hosted 10.8 million immigrants; France and Italy respectively 6.7 million and 4.5 million. (see: IOM, World Migration Report, 2010) While not all immigrants are necessarily non-white, the proportion of immigrants that are likely to be identified as such is non-trivial. Exact numbers are obviously not available, but proxies such as the country of origin confirm this. For instance, at the end of 2014, more than 1 million individuals with African origins were legally resident in Italy (official statistics available at: http://demo.istat.it/str2014/index.html. Forecasts suggest that these numbers are likely to increase in the next years due to the large scale

due to migratory fluxes that Europe is expected to experience in the coming years.[18] Significant demographic changes of this type may trigger (conscious and unconscious) negative reactions of the majoritarian racial group.[19] These reactions can add up to preexisting expressions of discrimination. One possible context in which discrimination can occur is the courtroom. In this connection, racial discrimination in criminal trials has been long studied in both psychology[20] and economics[21]. This literature offers evidence that members of racial minority groups are discriminated against in the criminal law systems of various Western countries. Conversely, research on the impact of race on tort trial outcomes is much more limited. Besides some anecdotal evidence,[22] only two quantitative studies have analyzed the presence of discrimination across racial/ethnic groups in these settings.[23] In line with the results obtained in criminal settings, both studies found that members of minority groups are discriminated against in civil trials. Similarly, with some exceptions,[24] there are very few studies concerned with the issue of gender discrimination in tort trials. This is surprising. Indeed tort law plays a key

---

immigration from Africa and the Middle-East (see: EPSC, Legal Migration in the EU, Issue 2, 2015).

18 EPSC, Legal Migration in the EU 2, 2015.

19 See for instance: Maureen Craig and Jennifer Richeson, 2014. More Diverse Yet Less Tolerant? How the Increasingly Diverse Racial Landscape Affects white Americans' Racial Attitudes. 40(6) PERS. SOC. PSYCHOL. BULL. 750.

20 For meta-analytical studies on existing literature on the subject see: Tara Mitchell et al., 2005. Racial Bias in Mock Juror Decision-making: a Meta-analytic Review of Defendant Treatment, 29 LAW HUM. BEHAV 627; Devine Dennis and Caughlin David 2014. Do They Matter? A Meta-Analytic Investigation of Individual Characteristics and Guilt Judgments (2014) 20(2) PSYCHOL. PUBLIC POLICY LAW. 109.

21 See Abrams David et al., 2012. Do Judges Vary in Their Treatment of Race?. THE JOURNAL OF LEGAL STUDIES, 41(2), 347; Gazal-Ayal Oren and Raanan Sulitzeanu-Kenan, 2010. Let My People Go: Ethnic In-Group Bias in Judicial Decisions—Evidence from a Randomized Natural Experiment. 7(3) J. EMPIR. LEG. STUD 403; Grossman Guy et al. 2016. Descriptive Representation and Judicial Outcomes in Multiethnic Societies. 60(1) AM. J. POLITICAL SCI 44.

22 For a discussion of racial discrimination in tort trials during the XIX and XX century in the US, see: Wriggins Jennifer, 2007. Damages in Tort Litigation: Thoughts on Race and Remedies, 1865-2007. 27(1) REVIEW OF LITIGATION 37. See also, generally: Chamallas Martha and Jennifer Wriggins. 2010. The Measure of Injury: Race, Gender, and Tort Law. NYU PRESS.

23 See Chin Audrey and Mark Peterson, 1985. Deep Pockets, Empty Pockets: Who Wins in Cook County Jury Trials, RAND REPORT; Shayo Moses and Asaf Zussman, 2011. Judicial Ingroup Bias in the Shadow of Terrorism 126(3) Q. J. ECON. 1447.

24 Chamallas Martha and Jennifer Wriggins, 2010. The Measure of an Injury: Race, Gender, and the Law of Torts. NYU PRESS.

role in regulating the conduct of individuals and private/public entities in a wide variety of settings such as environmental protection, consumer protection, and workplace safety.[25] This book aims to fill the knowledge gaps in this field and open a debate on these issues.

1.3 Limitations

As in any comparative legal study, I have limited the scope of the analysis to a restricted number of legal systems. As mentioned above, the focus is here on some European legal systems and on the US. I have included the US system because of the major role that American scholarship has in promoting the application of behavioral insights to law and policymaking. By expanding the analysis to European law, the book aims to circumscribe the scope of the analysis to a number of legal systems that, for historical reasons share common roots and that in more recent years have experienced forms of (attempted) harmonization under the umbrella of European integration.[26] The choice of these countries is therefore strategic from three perspectives.

First, similarities between countries make comparison more tractable. Second, this inquiry expands beyond a pure legal analysis to touch upon behavioral law and economics aspects of the functioning of different legal systems. As such, the present work can be seen as complementing well established strands of comparative legal research that focuses on European and the US legal systems.[27] Third, future harmonization attempts may benefit from this comparative analysis.

Nonetheless, to the extent that situations similar to those considered here prevail also in other legal systems, the informative scope of the analysis provided in this book can be extended beyond the countries explicitly considered here. In this

---

25 Generally, various streams of evidence indicate that private law plays an important role in determining inequalities among social groups. Sandefur Rebecca, 2008. Access to civil justice and race, class, and gender inequality. 34 ANNU. REV. SOCIOL 340.

26 See, for instance, the projects brought forward by the European Group on Tort Law (available at: http://www.egtl.org/) and the recent European Parliament study on the harmonization of European civil procedural law (available at: http://www.europarl.europa.eu/RegData/etudes/IDAN/2015/559499/EPRS_IDA(2015)559499_EN.pdf)

27 See, for instance, the well-established work that the European Centre of Tort and Insurance Law (http://www.ectil.org/) has produced in the last decades.

regard, it is worth nothing that many behavioral patterns highlighted by psychology and behavioral economics have (often strong) cross-country validity so that research conducted with citizens of one country often provides insights on the decision-making of citizens of other countries.[28] Research has also highlighted that there are sometimes exceptions to these uniform trends.[29] For this reason, throughout the book, I will discuss whether and to what extent the behavioral phenomena on which the analysis focuses is relevant also for the decision-making of the populations considered.

In addition, since each Chapter addresses a selected topic in tort and evidence law, the overarching issue of accuracy and behavioral law and economics is touched upon in a scattered manner. The book therefore does not aim to provide a definitive answer to the debates on the interplay between accuracy and behavioral law and economics. Instead, it discusses various issues related to this central topic, contributing to the debate on this topic from different angles.

Furthermore, the book has a strong empirical focus. When possible, I support theoretical arguments with empirical evidence and Chapter 3 provides some empirical evidence itself. Yet, for obvious reasons linked to the necessarily circumscribed scope of a book, I develop some of the issues discussed only at a theoretical level. Ideally, these theoretical arguments can set the basis for future empirical research in this field.

Lastly, a large part of the book is descriptive in nature. In this sense, the present work does not offer any definitive answer to normative questions related to tort and evidence law. Yet, as mentioned above, the book highlights how behavioral insights can be relevant to answer different normative questions that arise in relation to the regulation of these branches of the law. As such, the present work has clear policy relevance.

---

28 John Berry et al., 2002. Cross-cultural Psychology: Research and Applications. CAMBRIDGE UNIVERSITY PRESS.

29 Berry et al. (2002).

2 Truth Standards in Behavioral Law and Economics[30]

2.1 Introduction

Truth, in either one or both of its forms - accuracy and coherence - is widely considered a major aim of adjudication.[31] In legal scholarship, institutional settings are therefore often evaluated, compared, and sometimes reformed on the basis of whether they help and compel adjudicators to reach truthful decisions. These evaluations and reforms have often been informed by studies in judgment and decision-making (JDM) and with the relatively recent rise of behavioral law and economics, this trend is growing at a fast pace. Similar to adjudication, many studies in JDM assess the human competence to form judgments and decisions with reference to their ability to achieve truth.[32] Thus, trial settings are often evaluated and reformed on the basis of truth standard adopted in JDM. In this connection, as recently highlighted by Hammond and by a special edition of *Judgment and Decision Making*,[33] studies in JDM often adopt different truth standards. This Chapter argues that to the extent that legal scholarship relies on JDM to evaluate legal rules and practices, it should not ignore the differences in truth standards adopted in JDM.

Three main reasons support this claim: first, taking into account differences in truth standards adopted in JDM is sometimes important to identify whether a given behavioral phenomenon has to be considered problematic in light of the normative truth criterion used to assess adjudication. Second, as it will be shown below, JDM sometimes adopts questionable truth standards, which, if used to evaluate courts' performance, may not lead to improvements in, and maybe even

---

30 This Chapter is partially a reproduction of the following article: Goran Dominioni, Peter Desmet, and Louis Visscher, 2020, Judges Versus Jurors: Biased Attributions in the Courtroom, 52:1 CORNELL INTERNATIONAL LAW JOURNAL 102.

31 Michele Taruffo, 2014. Evidence, in M. Cappelletti eds, INTERNATIONAL ENCYCLOPEDIA OF COMPARATIVE LAW - CIVIL PROCEDURE VOL XVI.

32 Hammond Kenneth, 2007. Beyond Rationality: The Search for Wisdom in a Troubled Time. OXFORD UNIVERSITY PRESS.

33 Dunwoody Philip, 2009. Theories of Truth as Assessment Criteria in Judgment and Decision Making, 4(2) JUDGM. DECIS. MAK 116.

G. Dominioni, *Biased Trials*, Ökonomische Analyse des Rechts | Economic Analysis of Law, https://doi.org/10.1007/978-3-658-30080-7_2

worsen, adjudication. Third, depending on which truth criterium is adopted, the strength of the evidence supporting behavioral responses to determined policy failures changes. To the extent that behavioral law and economics is (or wants to be) an empirically driven field of research, this is a non-trivial issue.

To illustrate these points, the Chapter builds on studies of one of the most influential behavioral phenomena in legal scholarship, namely the fundamental attribution error (FAE). In addition, particular attention will be given to the use of truth standards to evaluate courts' performance in law and economics, which is one of the strands of legal scholarship that is more heavily influenced by behavioral insights. The focus will be on the economics of judicial errors in the imposition of liability, as most legal literature on the FAE focuses on this issue.

The Chapter is structured as follows: Section 2 discusses truth as a criterion to evaluate courts' decisions and human decision-making. Section 3 addresses the issues of truth in adjudication with regards to the imposition of liability in the economics of tort law. Section 4 discusses the problems that arise from mismatches between the psychological use of truth standards in experiments on the FAE and their interpretation in legal scholarship. Section 5 concludes.

2.2 Truth in Adjudication and JDM

Legal scholars generally agree on that truth is a main aim of adjudication.[34] From this perspective, procedural rules and practices should be shaped to nudge courts in establishing the truth of the facts considered.

Building on the epistemological debate on truth, legal scholars distinguish between two types of judicial truth that a legal system can aim to achieve: correspondence and coherence.[35] The focus of the correspondence theory is empirical truth. In this perspective, a court decision is true only when it corresponds to the empirical facts that occurred outside the trial.[36] The basic tenets of this theory are that facts are understandable and there is only one truth.[37] This seems the conception of truth that part of the law and economics scholarship adopts when discussing

34 For different perspectives on the aim of adjudication see: Louis Kaplow (2015); Mirjan Damaska, 1997. 49 Truth in adjudication. HASTINGS L.J. 289.

35 Taruffo (2014)

36 Ibid.

37 Ibid.

judicial errors (see below Section 3).[38] Correspondence is also the most ancient theory of truth among those that permeate the current debate on the philosophy of JDM and it is often seen as the closest to the common sense view of truth. In this view, a judgment is true only when it is factually (empirically) accurate and regardless of whether the cognitive process that led to the judgment could be somehow justified or even illustrated.[39]

The second, most prominent theory of truth in evidence law and JDM is coherence. The coherence theory of truth is more recent than the correspondence theory[40] and its central tenet is that facts as such are generally not knowable to humans because the understanding of facts is itself made through perception and judgment.[41] Since facts are only knowable trough senses, what we refer to as facts are beliefs themselves.[42] Given the impossibility to empirically assess the truthfulness of our beliefs, the way to establish truth is to determine the coherence of beliefs.[43] Thus, only a coherent set of beliefs can be said to be true.[44]

Coherence can refer to interpersonal coherence or intrapersonal coherence.[45] On the one hand, a set of beliefs held by a person can be said to be true from an intrapersonal perspective if, and only if, all its separate parts are consistent with one another.[46] For instance, in the field of JDM transitivity is an issue of intrapersonal coherence.[47] On the other hand, from an interpersonal point of view,

38 Garoupa and Rizzolli (2012)

39 Kenneth Hammond, 1996. Human Judgment and Social Policy: Irreducible Uncertainty, Inevitable Error, Unavailable Injustice, OXFORD UNIVERSITY PRESS, p. 106.

40 For a brief overview of the historical roots of coherence theory, see: Dawson Neal and Frederick Gregory, 2009). Correspondence and Coherence in Science: A Brief Historical Perspective. 4(2) JUDGM. DECIS. MAK 126.

41 Philip Dunwoody, 2009. Theories of Truth as Assessment Criteria in Judgment and Decision Making. 42(6) JUDGM. DECIS. MAK 116.

42 Ibid

43 Ibid.

44 Hammond (1996).

45 Dunwoody (2009).

46 Hammond (2009); Dunwoody (2009).

47 Transitivity refers to the fact that it would be incoherent for an individual to prefer x to y, y to z and not prefer x to z. See on this: Korobkin, Russell B., and Thomas Ulen, 2000. Law And Behavioral Science: Removing The Rationality Assumption From Law And Economics. 88 CAL. L. REV. 1051.

the beliefs of an individual are true only if they are consistent with the beliefs that are largely shared by other individuals.[48]

The assumption underlying the coherence theory is that truth cannot be inconsistent. However, the coherence theory does not imply that every set of coherent beliefs is necessarily true from a correspondence perspective, meaning that a set of coherent beliefs can be empirically inaccurate.[49] It is not clear when increases in coherence of beliefs triggers an increase in correspondence.[50] Thus, given that coherence is a necessary but not sufficient element of truth, it has been argued that truth requires both correspondence and coherence.[51] Generally, neither in JDM nor in legal scholarship there is agreement on which is/are the standard(s) of truth that should be adopted.[52] Yet, as I argue below, the economics of tort law seems to give more prominence to correspondence than to coherence as standards to evaluate courts' performance.

2.3 The Economic Value of Truth in the Imposition of Liability

Rationality in economics is defined according to coherence criteria.[53] A large part of law and economics assumes that judges make coherent decisions. For instance, Posner describes judges as Bayesian updaters in several of his writings.[54] Yet, in this context, coherence is adopted as a descriptive criterion and not as a normative one. This is because in law and economics truth is not seen per se as an independent goal of adjudication. Instead, the normative standard endorsed by this

48 Hammond (1996); Dunwoody (2009).

49 Dunwoody (2009).

50 Ibid.

51 Dunwoody (2009); Dawson and Gregory (2009).

52 Hammond (1996); Taruffo (2104); Susan Haack, 2014. Justice, Truth, and Proof: Not So Simple, After All.

53 Generally rational choice theory assumes that: 1) Individuals are able to compare goods and rank them according to their preferences (completeness); 2) Individuals rank alternative outcomes in a consistent way according to their preferences (transitivity, as defined above). 3) Individuals make choices considering the payoffs of their actions and not on the basis of how the choice is framed (invariance); 4) The choice between options should depend on the features that distinguish them (cancellation); 5) Between the option x and option y, and individual should always choose x when x is at least as good as y for every features and dominates y in at least one feature (dominance). See: Korobkin and Ulen (2000).

54 Ruchard Posner, 2010. How Judges Think. HARVARD UNIVERSITY PRESS.

strand of literature for the evaluation of legal systems is social welfare maximization. With specific regards to tort law, this aim is translated into the minimization of the social cost of accidents.[55] To the extent that the failure to make coherent decisions does not systematically increase the costs of accidents, neoclassical law and economics does not see it as a problem.[56] The same applies to correspondence. Yet, in this regard, law and economics scholars have long highlighted that correspondence in adjudication (often referred to as accuracy) is a major driver of social welfare maximization. To understand why, let us first briefly introduce the economic model of tort law.

When viewed through the lenses of economics, the primary aim of tort law is to incentivize potential tortfeasors and victims to make optimal investments in precautionary measures. This aim is achieved by allocating the expected losses of the accident between the tortfeasor and the victim.[57] Since the discussion of the economic model of tort law is here merely instrumental to illustrate the relevance of truth criteria in assessing courts' performance, the discussion is here limited to unilateral accidents. Unilateral accidents are those where only injurers can influence the probability and the magnitude of the loss. In this framework, according to the marginal Hand formula this allocation should take place so that the tortfeasor has an incentive to take optimal care. Optimal care is the level of care at which marginal cost of taking care equals the marginal benefit from the reduction in expected accident losses. When the injurers' level of activity is taken into account, the goal of tort law becomes to maximize the utility that injurers derive from carrying out their activities less the sum of the expected damages of accidents and the costs of avoiding accidents.[58] The increase in utility that an injurer enjoys from engaging in the activity an additional time is referred to as the marginal utility of the activity. Conversely, the cost of avoiding accidents is equal to the product of

---

55 Guido Calabresi, 1970. The Cost of Accidents: A Legal and Economic Analysis. New Haven; London: YALE UNIVERSITY PRESS.

56 The argument made here is not that incoherent judgments never lead decreases in social welfare. More simply, my point is that the link between these two elements is not necessarily obvious, especially when one considers the large variety of coherence criteria that can be adopted to evaluate human judgments.

57 Steven Shavell, 1987. Economic Analysis of Accident Law. HARVARD UNIVERSITY PRESS, Cambridge.

58 Shavell (1987).

the level of activity and the level of care.[59] In this context, social welfare is maximized when the marginal utility that injurer derives from engaging an additional time in their activity equals the sum of the increase of the cost of taking due care and the increase in the expected accident losses.[60] In absence of tort law injurers may have an incentive to engage too much in their activity.[61] This is because the additional risk created by increases in activity levels would not be internalized.[62] The economic aim of tort law is to remedy to this market failure by imposing optimal deterrence.[63]

Legal economists have long highlighted the importance of accuracy (read correspondence) in the establishment of liability for the achievement of optimal deterrence.[64] Accuracy is here defined as the degree by which courts commit false positive (or type I) errors – i.e. they impose liability on individuals that did not violate a legal command – and false negative (or type II) errors - i.e. they do not impose liability on individuals that did violate a legal command.[65]

The basic mechanism via which accuracy is related to deterrence was first described by Png in 1986 and it goes as follows[66]: ceteris paribus, improvements in accuracy increase the cost of committing a tortious act and decrease the cost of not committing it.[67] To see why this is the case imagine a legal system in which sanctions are imposed randomly. Here, the expected liability of an individual is independent from whether - and to what extent - he engages in a potentially tortious activity. Therefore, the legal system does not provide any incentive to individuals not to engage in an activity. Starting from this situation, a shift from this

59 Schäfer Hans-Bernd and Frank Müller-Langer, 2009. Strict Liability Versus Negligence. In Tort Law and Economics, EDWARD ELGAR.

60 Shavell (1987).

61 Shavell (2004).

62 Ibid.

63 Ibid.

64 Png Ivan, 1986. Optimal Subsidies and Damages in the Presence of Judicial Error. 6(1) INT. REV. LAW ECON 101; Louis Kaplow, 1994. The Value of Accuracy in Adjudication: An Economic Analysis. 23(1) J. LEG. STUD. 345. Notice that accuracy in adjudication does not have similar importance for other types of decisions made in tort trials. This is the case for instance with regards to damages awards, where only average accuracy matters. See on this: Louis Kaplow and Steven Shavell, 1996. Accuracy in the Assessment of Damages. J.L. & ECON, 39(1), 191-210.

65 Kaplow (1994).

66 Png (1986).

67 Kaplow (1994).

state of the world to one in which courts are more likely to impose liability on subjects that have committed a tort than on those that did not, will increase the cost of engaging in tortious activities. In addition, reductions in false positives will decrease the expected liability of those that act in accordance with the legal command.

This conclusion has been questioned by Lando,[68] who distinguishes between wrongful convictions based on errors of acts and errors of identity. The former occur when a person is made liable for a tort that has actually not occurred (e.g. if no harm was caused). The second type of wrongful convictions takes place when a person is made liable instead of someone else. According to Lando, errors of identity are often unlikely to decrease deterrence because in this case both tortfeasors and non-tortfeasors can suffer liability for the mistake of the judge, for this reason none of them have an incentive to change behavior.

Garoupa and Rizzolli argue that Lando's perspective captures the effect of wrongful convictions only in a limited set of circumstances.[69] This is because for each wrongful imposition of liability, a tortfeasor escapes liability. In addition, the probability of being wrongfully made liable is higher for tortfeasors than for non-tortfeasors as, for instance, they may engage in the potentially tortious activity more than non-tortfeasors. From this it follows that the wrongful imposition of liability decreases the expected liability of committing a tort and increase the expected liability of not committing one.

Lando and Mungan contest this view.[70] In particular, they argue that there are various situations in which a wrongful imposition of liability does not necessarily lead to a missed imposition of liability to the actual tortfeasor. This occurs, for instance, when both the actual and the wrong tortfeasors are made liable.[71] In addition, Lando and Mungan argue that also for wrongful imposition of liability based on act, Png's theory fails to describe the effect of accuracy on deterrence for two reasons. First, under a negligence rule, a tortfeasor that takes due care but anticipates the possibility of being wrongfully made liable receives an incentive to increase investments in precautions. Thus type I errors may increase deterrence. In addition, if the probability of type I and II errors is conditional on adjudication,

68 Henrik Lando, 2006. Does Wrongful Conviction Lower Deterrence? 35(2) J. LEG. STUD. 327.

69 Garoupa and Rizzolli (2012).

70 Lando Henrik and Murat Mungan, 2018. The Effect of Type-1 Error On Deterrence. 53 INT. REV. LAW ECON 1.

71 Ibid.

type I errors affect deterrence less than type II errors. This holds as long as adjudication is more likely when the injurer has acted in violation of the law than otherwise. Thus, overall, according to Lando and Mungan, Type I errors related to acts may either increase deterrence or reduce it less than type II errors.

Overall, this brief overview of the current economic debate on accuracy in tort trials highlights that, with some qualification, there is general consensus that accuracy in adjudication affects deterrence, which in turn affects the production of social welfare. Thus, in the context of the economics of liability law correspondence is a primary criterion to evaluate the performance of judges. Indeed, Kaplow recently argues that if perfect accuracy could be achieved at no cost, social welfare maximization could be achieved by focusing exclusively on courts' accuracy.[72] Conversely, coherence in adjudication has a less manifest goal in the minimization of the social costs of accidents.

Having clarified the role of truth in adjudication from the perspective of the imposition of liability in law and in law and economics, the next section illustrates how ignoring differences in truth standards adopted in JDM can lead legal analysis astray. I elaborate this point by building on a specific branch of behavioral literature referred to as attribution theory.

2.4 An Example: Truth Standards and Attribution in Legal Scholarship

Attribution theory, i.e. the study of how individuals explain the events that they witness, is one of the theories in psychology that has been more widely applied to judicial decision-making. Conventionally, scholars identify the work of Heider as a cornerstone in the studies on attribution.[73] Heider was interested in analyzing how individuals understand the world that surrounds them. According to Heider, the behavior of a person is the result of two variables: the person and the situation.[74] Thus, a person that aims to understand the determinants of human behavior has to find a method to distinguish the causal contribution of each of the two variables.

72 Kaplow (2015).

73 See, for instance: Harold Kelley, 1973. The Process of Causal Attribution, 28(2) AM. PSYCHOL 107.

74 Fritz Heider, 1958. The Psychology of Interpersonal Relations. NEW YORK: WILEY.

Within attribution theory, legal scholars have given particular attention to the Fundamental Attribution Error (FAE), which refers to the human tendency to underestimate the power of situational factors and overestimate the influence of dispositional factors in causing human behavior.[75] This Section discusses the use of truth standards in the study of the FAE and the (mis)use of these studies to evaluate the functioning of trial systems.

2.4.1 Correspondence and Coherence in Attribution

The starting point of this analysis is that the use of the terms overestimation/underestimation in the definition of the FAE implies the existence of a reference point from which the estimation is made. In addition, the qualification of the FAE as a judgment that does not correspond to the truth implies that this reference point has to be a truthful one. Following Hammond,[76] Dunwoody[77] and Jennings,[78] this Section discusses correspondence and the various coherence criteria adopted in the context of attribution theory.

2.4.1.1 Correspondence in Attribution

As discussed above, correspondence focuses on empirical truth. Attribution theorists often consider the issue of correspondence as a troubled one.[79] Determining the empirical accuracy of causal attributions requires first to be able to determine the empirically true determinants of human behavior, however the latter are difficult to establish.[80]

Ross argues that despite the difficulties of determining the true causes of human behavior, it is still possible to establish the accuracy of attributions when the attributer is asked to predict the behavior of others.[81] In these cases, the accuracy of the attribution could be determined by comparing the prediction with the actual

---

75 Lee Ross, 1977. The Intuitive Psychologist and His Shortcomings: Distortions in the Attribution Process. 10 ADVANCES IN EXPERIMENTAL SOCIAL PSYCHOLOGY 173.

76 Hammond (2007).

77 Dunwoody (2009).

78 Kyle Jennings, 2010. Coherent Attributions with Co-occurring and Interacting Causes, PHD THESIS UNIVERSITY OF CALIFORNIA, Berkeley.

79 See for instance: David Funder, 1987. Errors and Mistakes: Evaluating the Accuracy of Social Judgment, 101 (1) PSYCHOL. BULL

80 Jennings (2010).

81 Ross (1977).

(observed) behaviors.[82] For instance, psychologists have often devised experiments in which a pool of participants was asked to predict the behavior of other participants in presence and absence of some situational factor. The analysis was aimed to understand and test whether the predictions matched the observed behavior in the two conditions, i.e. whether participants could predict the behavioral influence of the situational factor.[83]

2.4.1.2 Coherence in Attribution Theory

Attribution theorists have prevalently used coherence as theory of truth.[84] Most of these theories adopted an intrapersonal definition of coherence, and only few of them grounded their normative standard of reference into an external logical system.[85] This section begins with introducing some of the earlier theories of attribution and some of the key concepts in attribution theory. Subsequently it discusses two of the most influential normative theories of attribution. These normative criteria are used below as benchmarks for the evaluation of empirical findings on the FAE.

A normative theory of attribution aims to illustrate when and by how much individuals ought to discount the causal contribution of one factor to an event in presence of an alternative plausible cause. Thus, for instance, a normative theory of attribution elaborates on how a judge should infer the presence of a human error from the observation of an accident when an alternative plausible situational cause of the accident is present (eg. a mechanical failure).[86] Notice that, here, the judge is trying to establish what is the plausible causal contribution to the occurrence of an event (the accident), of two probabilistically independent sufficient causes (the human error and the mechanical failure). In order to establish a normative standard for discounting, attribution theories address two main issues:[87] 1) When an individual should discount; 2) What is the right amount of discounting.

---

82 Causal judgment of an observed behavior and prediction of behavior are not strictly speaking the same task, nonetheless they are strongly interdependent. Ross (1977).

83 For a detailed description of some of these experiments see below Section 4.2.

84 Jennings (2010).

85 Ibid.

86 Morris Michael and Richard Larrick, 1995. When One Cause Casts Doubt on Another: A Normative Analysis of Discounting in Causal Attribution. 102(2) PSYCHOL. REV, 331.

87 Morris and Larrick (1995).

With regards to when to discount, in a seminal work that builds on Heider's framework,[88] Kelley argues that discounting for one cause should occur when another plausible cause is also present.[89] Thus, a judge should be less convinced that the cause of the accident under scrutiny at trial was a negligent conduct of the driver when the expert testimony highlights a mechanical failure in the brakes of the car. This, rather intuitive, finding has been upheld by subsequent normative studies.[90]

In addition, in relation to how much to discount, Kelley makes a positive statement that describes the behavior observed in laboratory experiments according to which subjects do not attribute an effect (e.g., behavior) to a causal factor (e.g., disposition) when another sufficiently strong plausible cause (e.g., situation) of the same effect is also present.[91] Surprisingly, this positive statement has been subsequently adopted as a normative criterion of attribution.[92] In 1977 Ross writes that the discounting principle can be described as follows: "To the extent that situational or external factors constitute a "sufficient" explanation for an event, that event is attributed to the situation and no inference logically can be made (and, presumably, no inference empirically is made) about the disposition of the actor"[93]. Hereafter I will refer to this argument as to Ross's criterion. Gilbert and Malone describe this normative criterion as the attribution theory's fundamental rule of logic.[94]

Following this earlier contributions, other authors have discussed criteria according to which individuals should rationally discount.[95] Among these, a widely known normative theory of attribution has been proposed by Morris and Larrick

---

88 Heider's work has set the basis for the development of various theories of attribution. See for instance: Bernard Weiner, 1985. An Attributional Theory of Achievement Motivation and Emotion. 92(4) PSYCHOL REV. 548. In this section I focus on those that are more relevant for the present discussion.

89 Ibid.

90 Ibid.

91 Ibid.

92 Funder (1987).

93 Ross (1977).

94 Gilbert and Malone (1995).

95 See for instance, Ajzen Icek and Martin Fishbein, 1975. A Bayesian Analysis of Attribution Processes, 82(2) PSYCHOL. BULL, 261.

(hereafter Morris and Larrick's criterion).[96] This model addresses both the questions of when and to what extent discounting of one cause is normatively warranted when another plausible cause of an observed behavior is present.[97] Building on Kelley's model, Morris and Larrick answer the question regarding "when to discount" as follows: the probability of a particular cause of a behavior being present should be discounted when another cause is also present.[98]

The second issue that this model addresses regards the amount by which the presence of a particular cause of an event (i.e. an accident) should be discounted given the presence of another cause. In this regard, they argue that the right amount of discounting depends on the attributor's prior probability that a certain cause is present (e.g. a mechanical failure) given the observation of the event (e.g. the accident).[99] The lower is this probability and the more the observation of the cause calls for discounting. For instance, let's consider two versions of a stylized world. In one version of this world (A), judges believe that mechanical failures and negligence driving account only for 10% of the accidents, respectively. Therefore, when informed that an accident has occurred, they think that there are 10% probability that a mechanical failure has caused it and 10% probability than the negligent behavior of the driver was the actual cause. In another version of this world (B), judges think that mechanical failures cause 20% of the accidents and an equal probability applies to negligent driving. Imagine now that an expert testimony provides evidence that a mechanical failure has occurred in relation to an accident under scrutiny at trial. Here, judges in world A should discount more that probability that the driver was negligent than in world B. This is because in world A, mechanical failures are less frequent than in world B.[100]

Attribution theorists have widely adopted the truth theories illustrated above to determine whether and under which circumstances humans overestimate the role that dispositional factors have in shaping human behavior, i.e. to study the prevalence of the FAE in a given population. Following Jennings[101] the next section illustrates how empirical findings on the FAE can be interpreted on the basis

---

96 Morris and Larrick (1995).

97 Ibid.

98 Ibid.

99 Notice that this model provides a normative standard that allows testing only for internal consistency of beliefs.

100 Ibid. Morris and Larrick (1995).

101 Jennings (2010).

of these coherence-based theories of truth and the correspondence theory of truth accepted in attribution theory.

2.4.2 Overestimation and Underestimation: Empirical Studies on the Fundamental Attribution Error and Their Interpretation

This section illustrates some of the studies that are used to support the existence of the FAE. This review does not aim at completeness, conversely attention is given to the studies that are most often cited in the legal literature on the FAE and tort law.

2.4.2.1 The Milgram's Experiment

A first study that is often interpreted as showing the existence of the FAE is the Milgram's study on obedience.[102] As I will discuss below, this experiment does not deal directly with explaining an observed behavior. Conversely, it focuses on predicting future behaviors. As explained above, within attribution theory, testing the accuracy of predictions is considered a meaningful way to determine the accuracy of judgement.

In the Milgram's study participants were asked to take a role in an experiment that was allegedly aimed to improve both the learning capacity and the memory skills of another person through the use of punishment.[103] Participants had to take the part of the "teacher", while an actor that pretended to be a subject to the experiment took the part of the "learner".[104] The learner had to memorize a set of pairing words. During the experiment the teacher was required to mention one word of the pair and the learner had to recall the associated word.[105] When the answer provided by the learner was correct, the teacher had to verbally reward the learner.[106] Conversely, when the learner answer was wrong, the teacher was asked to punish him by delivering an electric shock.[107] The teacher delivered the shock by pushing a lever on an apparatus connected to the body of the learner.[108] At the first mistake

---

102 Philip Zimbardo, 2007. Lucifer Effect. BLACKWELL PUBLISHING LTD.

103 Ibid.

104 Ibid.

105 Ibid.

106 Ibid.

107 Ibid.

108 Ibid.

made by the learner, the delivered shock was of 15 w. At each additional error the intensity of the shock increased by 15 w, up to 450 w.[109] Of course, the electric shocks delivered were not real ones.[110] Nonetheless, the actor pretended to receive pain from the punishment. Depending on the degree of punishment received, the learner could start complaining about the pain, ask to stop the experiment, scream and at higher levels of punishment pretending to have lost his senses. [111]

Milgram asked 40 US psychiatrists to predict how many of the subjects in the role of teachers would have accepted to deliver shocks for each level of punishment.[112] The average prediction was that most people would have refused to deliver the shock at 150 w and that only 1 out of 1000 (the sadists) would have gone all the way up to 450 w.[113] The actual result from the Milgram experiment shows that 65% of the participants went on up to the maximum level of punishment.[114] The participants to the experiment themselves did not predict that they would have behaved as such.[115]

From a correspondence perspective, the prediction made by both the participants to the experiment and third parties are mistaken because they do not match the actual behavior observed in the experiment. As mentioned above, studies on the accuracy of prediction of behavior do not directly address the causal judgment issue, nonetheless the two types of judgment are greatly interdependent.[116] Thus, these results are interpreted as showing the existence of the FAE because the failure to predict the behavior of teachers would be due to an underestimation of the power of situational factors (the requests of the experimenter) and an overestimation of the dispositional factors (unwillingness to harm the learner) in determining teachers' behavior.[117] These findings are one of the few that provide information regarding the accuracy of human general theories on human nature, i.e. they assess

109 Ibid.
110 Ibid.
111 Ibid.
112 Ibid.
113 Ibid.
114 Ibid.
115 Ross (1977).
116 Ibid.
117 Zimbardo (2007).

whether a set of attributions are true from a correspondence perspective.[118] However, they leave open the question of which is the correct ratio between dispositional and situational attribution, i.e. these studies provide no guidance regarding whether attributions are coherent.

2.4.2.2 The Quiz Game Experiment

In another experiment widely cited to support the existence of the FAE subjects participated in a quiz game.[119] Participants were randomly assigned in two different groups: the members of one group (the questioners) were required to ask questions to the other group (the contestants).[120] The questions were general-knowledge type questions formulated by the questioners themselves. Contestants were asked to correctly answer the questions but usually failed in answering some of them.[121] Another group of subjects was asked to witness the experiment and rate the general knowledge of both groups.[122] Despite knowing that subjects had been randomly assigned to the two groups, observers rated the questioners as more knowledgeable than the contestants.[123] In addition, both contestants and the questioners themselves rated questioners as more knowledgeable than contestants.[124]

From a coherence perspective this experiment may show the existence of the FAE. As mentioned above, one of the earlier and most widely accepted normative canons (Ross' canon) of attribution.[125] In this case the sufficient explanation for the relative performance of the two groups should have been found in the ad-

---

118 Denis Hilton, 2013. Causal Explanation: From Social Perception to Knowledge-Based Attribution, in SOCIAL PSYCHOLOGY: HANDBOOK OF BASIC PRINCIPLES, A.W. Kruglanski and E.T. Higgins Eds., 246.

119 Roger Sumpton and Mick Gregson, 1981. The Fundamental Attribution Error: An Investigation Of Sensitivity To Role-Conferred Advantages In Self-Presentation. 20:1 BRITISH JOURNAL OF SOCIAL PSYCHOLOGY 7.

120 Ibid.

121 Ibid.

122 Ibid.

123 Ibid.

124 Ibid.

125 Ross (1977).

vantage of questioners over contestants given by the auto-selection of the questions by the questioners.[126] Thus, if we adopt the abovementioned standard as normative, the fact that the questioners were evaluated as having a broader general knowledge than the contestants has to be interpreted as an underestimation of the situational factors in determining human conduct. However, this experiment does not provide insights regarding whether attributions were accurate.

2.4.2.3 The Castro Essay Experiment

In a third, often cited, experiment used to support the existence of the FAE individuals were asked to write either a pro- or an anti- Castro essays (in other versions of this experiment on the legalization of marijuana).[127] Other subjects to the experiments were then asked to read these essays.[128] The readers were informed that the writers had been paid to write the essay and that the assignment either to pro-Castro or anti-Castro positions had been random.[129] Subsequently, readers were asked to declare the extent by which they believed that the author of the essay they had read had either a pro- or an anti-Castro attitude.[130] Subjects who had read pro-Castro essays rated the authors of the pro-Castro essays as more pro-Castro compared to the subjects who had read anti-Castro essays.[131]

From a correspondence point of view, the Castro essay experiment supports the existence of the FAE.[132] In some version of this experiment, writers were first asked to state their opinion on Castro (legalization of marijuana).[133] The attributions made by the readers were subsequently matched with those of the writers.[134] The results show that attributions were significantly more in line with the content of the essay than with the actual opinion of the writers.[135] This suggests that the

---

126 Ibid.

127 Jones Edward and Victor Harris, 1967. The Attribution of Attitudes. 3(1) J. EXP. SOC. PSYCHOL 1.

128 Ibid.

129 Ibid.

130 Ibid.

131 Ibid.

132 Glenn Reeder, 1982. Let's Give the Fundamental Attribution Error Another Chance, 43(2) J PERS. SOC. PSYCHOL 341.

133 Snyder Melvin and Edward Jones, 1974. Attitude Attribution when Behavior is Constrained. 10 J. EXP. SOC. PSYCHOL 585.

134 Ibid.

135 Ibid.

readers failed to take into account the situational pressure that the request of the experimenter had on writers' essay.[136]

Conversely, from a coherence perspective, whether the Castro essay experiment shows inconsistency of belief is not straightforward, because it depends on how consistency is defined. According to the widely accepted normative criteria of attribution illustrated above, subjects should not infer dispositional traits from an observed behavior when the conduct can be explained by the presence of a sufficiently strong situational factor.[137] In the Castro essay experiment the sufficient explanation is identified with the request of the experimenter to write either a pro- or an anti- Castro essay. Therefore, given the existence of a sufficient explanation for the essay, no inference should have been logically made about the true opinion of the writer. Thus, given that readers' inferences regarding the true attitude of the writers seemed to be influenced by the content of the essay they had read, the existence of the FAE would have been shown.

Nonetheless, a change in the normative canon of attribution may lead to a different conclusion. Morris and Larrick repeated the original Castro essay experiment with a variation.[138] The variation consisted in asking readers to declare their beliefs regarding the probability that: 1) A pro-Castro person would have been assigned to write a pro-Castro essay; 2) A person that is instructed to write a pro-Castro essay would comply with the request.[139] These data were gathered before and after the readers read the essay. Only after having gathered these data the reader was made aware of the fact that writers had been constrained (through the request of the experimenter), in their choice regarding whether to write a pro- or an anti- Castro essay.[140] After this disclosure, readers were asked to indicate their belief that the author of the essay was a pro-Castro person. With these data Morris and Larrick analyzed the internal consistency of the belief of the readers by applying the normative canon of attribution developed by themselves in 1995.[141] Their findings showed that reader's belief were almost perfectly internally consistent.[142]

136 Ibid.

137 Ross (1977).

138 Morris and Larrick (1995).

139 Ibid.

140 Ibid.

141 Ibid.

142 Ibid.

In other words, the attributions made by the subjects were perfectly consistent with the normative criteria tested.

Thus, overall, attributions that are considered as true under one coherence criterion are not necessarily true under another. As it is explained below, this discrepancy of results regarding the human competence to make true attributions is often ignored in legal scholarship.

2.4.3 The Fundamental Attribution Error in Legal Scholarship

The empirical studies examined in the previous pages had an important impact on the positive and normative study of tort law as well as other branches of the law. This influence is manifest when reviewing the legal literature on the FAE.

This scholarship has focused mainly on criminal law and tort law. In the tort law sphere, various authors highlight how the FAE leads to unjust and inefficient determination of causation.[143] For instance, Levinson and Peng argue that the FAE unduly increases the set of circumstances in which a defendant is likely to be regarded as the cause of a harm.[144] This in turn, may prevent tort law from achieving fairness and optimal deterrence. Similarly, Prentice discusses the role of the FAE in determining investors' compensation in securities fraud law and argues that it is likely that this phenomenon leads to inaccurate findings with regards to the causation requirement.[145] Along these lines, Quintanilla argues that the FAE may lead courts to too easily find intention in the application of federal security law.[146] Because of this, managers are unjustly made liable for their unintentional actions. In addition, Feigenson warns that experienced lawyers may take advantage of courts' propensity to commit the FAE to favour their clients.[147] European tort law scholars are not foreign to literature on the FAE. Giard argues that because of the FAE, obstetricians are exposed to a too high level of liability as they are accused of

143 Levinson Justin and Kaiping Peng, 2004. Different Torts for Different Cohorts: A Cultural Psychological Critique of Tort Law's Actual Cause and Foreseeability Inquiries, 13(2) SOUTH. CALIF. INTERDISCIP. LAW J. 195; Robert Prentice, 2012. Behavioral Economics Applied: Loss Causation. 44 LOYOLA UNIVERSITY CHICAGO LAW JOURNAL 1509.

144 Levinson and Peng (2004).

145 Prentice (2012).

146 Victor Quintanilla, 2011. (Mis)judging Intent: The Fundamental Attribution Error in Federal Securities Law, 7 N.Y.U. J. L. & BUS 195.

147 Neal Feigenson, 1995. The Rhetoric of Torts: How Advocates Help Jurors Think About Causation, Reasonableness, and Responsibility. 47 HASTINGS L. J. 61.

losses that they could have not prevented.[148] Similarly, Giesen[149] discusses the role of the FAE in relation to the determination of causation and argues that it may lead to inaccuracies in fact finding. Similar conclusions have been recently put forward by Graziadei.[150]

A recent strand of literature on the FAE in tort relates to the debate on the role of race and gender at trial as various studies have shown that people are more prone to commit the FAE when observing negative behaviors of outgroup members than when confronted with unwarranted conducts of ingroup members.[151] In particular, Chamallas and Wriggins argue that the development of tort law remedies (for instance, what type of conducts are susceptible to give rise to a right to compensation), is unduly skewed by courts' propensity to commit the FAE in favour of males.[152] Similar claims have been recently proposed by Bussani and Infantino in explaining the role of culture in the development of tort law.[153]

Part of the legal scholarship on the FAE has taken a radical step in highlighting the relevance of this phenomenon for the study of tort law. This literature - which builds on the highly debated strand of psychology referred to as situationism[154] - "[i]s premised on the social scientific insight that the naïve psychology—that is, the highly simplified, affirming, and widely held model for understanding human thinking and behaviour - on which our laws and institutions are based is largely wrong"[155]. Situationists' main claim is that current legal scholarship in general, and the law and economics' rational actor model in particular, is built on

---

148 Raimond Giard, 2013. Birth-Related Brain Injuries: Torts in Trouble.

149 Ivo Giesen, 2012. Attribution, Legal Causation and Preventive Effects, in Judicial Decision Making in Civil Law, ELEVEN INTERNATIONAL PUBLISHING.

150 Michele Graziadei, 2009. What Went Wrong? Tort Law, Personal Responsibility, Expectations of Proper Care and Compensation. In European Tort Law. SPRINGER VIENNA.

151 Thomas Pettigrew, 1979. The Ultimate Attribution Error: Extending Allport's Cognitive Analysis of Prejudice. 5(4) PERS. SOC. PSYCHOL. BULL 461.

152 Chamallas and Wriggins (2010).

153 Mauro Bussani and Marta Infantino, 2015. Tort Law and Legal Cultures. 63(1) AM. J. COMP. L. 77.

154 Kenneth Bowers, 1973. Situationism in Psychology: An Analysis and a Critique. 80(5) PSYCHOL REV., 307; Philip G. Zimbardo, 2004. A Situationist Perspective on the Psychology of Evil: Understanding How Good People Are Transformed into Perpetrators. The Social Psychology of Good and Evil, 21, New York, NY, US: THE GUILFORD PRESS; Endler Norman and David Magnusson, 1976. Toward an Interactional Psychology of Personality. 83(5) PSYCHOL. BULL, 956.

155 Hanson Jon and Michael McCann, 2008. Situationist Torts, 41 LOYOLA OF LOS ANGELES LAW REVIEW 1359.

an erroneous conception of the determinants of human behavior, which ignores the crucial role that situations play in shaping behavior. Starting from these premises, Hanson and McCann argue that the human tendency to deny the appropriate role played by situations in determining human conduct may have contributed to produce an unjust tort law system in which, for instance, smokers bear the harm of their smoking habits despite corporations largely influence these habits through advertisement.[156] Hanson and McCann bring their reasoning a step further. According to their thesis, cigarette producers consciously take advantage of the existence of the FAE by advertising smoking as an expression of freedom, thus spreading the idea that smokers freely choose to smoke.[157] This, in turn, would influence court's perception of the determinants of smoking behavior and thus indirectly affect the attribution of liability in cigarettes related tort law cases to the advantage of producers.[158] Part of this scholarship goes so far as to argue that to avoid inaccuracies due to the FAE, we should reform the way in which tort law is taught in law school. In particular, Hanson and McCann propose a situationist model of teaching tort law that is alternative to the standard Langdellian model which focuses mainly on training law students in applying legal rules and principles to new situations.[159] In their view a tort law course should also teach students to look for situational forces that shape human behavior.[160]

In criminal law, Dripps argues that the FAE is a key factor in the development of various criminal doctrines.[161] For instance, he claims that the wider scope of the duress defence compared to necessity is due to the fact that the former prevents the defendant from being punished by blaming another person.[162] Conversely, necessity achieves the same outcome but in instances in which only situational factors could be blamed.[163] Dripps argues that it is because of the FAE and the consequential need to blame a person for the crime which explains the broader applicability of duress compared to necessity.[164] On a normative level, he invites

156 Ibid.

157 Ibid.

158 Ibid.

159 Hanson and McCann (2008).

160 Ibid.

161 Donald Dripps, 2003. Fundamental Retribution Error: Criminal Justice and the Social Psychology of Blame. VAND L REV, 56, 1383.

162 Ibid.

163 Ibid.

164 Ibid.

considering the FAE as one of the main risks for legal decision-making and proposes, for instance, that legislators should be more attentive to acquittals based on defences that redirect the blame towards a person than of those in which non-human factors justify or excuse the conduct of the defendant.[165] Along these lines, Ross and Shestowsky maintain, for instance, that dispositionism (i.e the tendency to attribute one's behavior to his/her disposition) among adjudicators over-restricts the scope for the recognition of mitigating circumstances that would warrant a more lenient treatment of criminal defendants.[166] Similarly, Koppel and Fondacaro argue that the FAE is one of the causes of retributivism and hard punishments in criminal settings.[167]

Lastly, studies on the FAE have been used by legal scholars to propose debiasing strategies, i.e. policies that aim to improve the decision-making of the individual without foreclosing her ability to make a decision. For instance, it has been argued that a potential debiasing strategy for the FAE is to make a judge accountable.[168] The use of accountability as a debiasing strategy for the FAE is based on Tetlock's study of 1985.[169] Tetlock's experiment shows that individuals that expect to be called to motivate their judgment regarding a particular behavior before witnessing it, are less likely than others to infer dispositional traits from the observed behavior.[170] These results have been interpreted as indicating that accountability induces individuals "to process social information in a more analytic and complex way and that can check judgmental biases such as… the fundamental attribution error"[171].

2.4.5 Fundamental Attribution Error in Legal Scholarship: Truth Related Issues

The previous section has illustrated the widespread use that legal scholarship has made of studies on the FAE. Most of the legal literature on tort law and the FAE

165 Ibid.

166 Lee Ross and Donna Shestowsky, 2002. Contemporary Psychology's Challenges to Legal Theory and Practice. 97 NW. U. L. REV 1081.

167 Koppel Stephen and Mark Fondacaro, 2016. The Retribution Heuristic. THE ROUTLEDGE HANDBOOK OF CRIMINAL JUSTICE ETHICS 191.

168 Giesen (2010).

169 Philip Tetlock, 1985. Accountability: A Social Check of the Fundamental Attribution Error, 48(3) SOC. PSYCHOL. Q, 227.

170 Ibid.

171 Tetlock (1985).

tend to discuss this phenomenon in a correspondence perspective.[172] Nonetheless, others explicitly refer to the FAE as a judgment that does not correspond to some normative canon of attribution.[173] This section argues that both strands of legal scholarship have sometimes failed to take due account of differences between the coherence-based and the correspondence based interpretations of studies on the FAE. On the basis of this analysis, I argue that this lack of attention is undesirable for the development of behavioral law and economics for at least three main reasons.

First, depending on which truth criterion one adopts to evaluate a given trial setting, the literature on the FAE may or may not highlight the existence of a problem. This is particularly true for scholars that support coherence as the criterion to assess judges' performance. Indeed, whether and to what extent the literature on the FAE highlights an issue that should be considered problematic, depends on the normative criterion of attribution adopted. This applies, for instance, with regards to the Castro essay experiment. As explained above, depending on the normative criterion of attribution adopted, the Castro essay experiment may (if one adopts Ross's criterion) or may not (if one adopts Morris and Larrik's criterion) highlight a failure to reason coherently. Failing to recognize this may lead to arguments weakly supported empirically.

The same applies for scholars that think that the only relevant truth criterion to assess procedural law is correspondence. Here, for instance, the evidence arising from the Quiz experiment is relevant solely to the extent that increases in coherence (under Ross's criterion) lead to improvements in correspondence. Yet, part of the literature seems to ignore this issue. In this regard, an important example are situationists. For instance, Benforado and Hanson propose a radical reform of tort law and the way in which it should be taught in law school by making reference to the substantial amount of evidence supporting the existence of the FAE.[174] In doing so, they discuss the literature that employs the Quiz Game paradigm, which, as explained above supports the existence of the FAE merely from the perspective of some normative theory of attribution.[175] Similarly, with regards to legal scholarship that builds on economic insights, Levinson and Peng argue that the

---

172 Hanson and Yosifon (2003); Levinson and Peng (2004).

173 Giesen (2010).

174 Adam Benforado and Jon Hanson, 2008. The Great Attributional Divide: How Divergent Views of Human Behavior Are Shaping Legal Policy, 57 EMORY L.J., 311.

175 Ibid.

evidence gathered in the Quiz essay experiment suggests that the influence of the FAE on courts' decisions may lead to the wrongful establishment of causation and prevent the achievement of optimal deterrence.[176] Yet, given what is discussed above it is not evident that the Quiz experiment can tell something about the ability of judges to make accurate decisions.

Second, some scholar argues that we should require judges to decide cases following normative theories of attribution.[177] As discussed above, attribution theorists have elaborated a number of normative theories of attribution with the aim of improving previous normative models. Each of these models proposes a different normative rule according to which attributors should perceive the determinants of human behavior. Thus, without a specification of which normative theory of attribution we should require judges to follow, the claim that judges should make decisions according to one these theories is empty. Before suggesting changes in the tort law system based on a departure from a normative model of judgment, it would be necessary to indicate the model at which reference is made to and make a case for requiring judges to follow this particular model. Nonetheless, it might be difficult to do so because even among attribution theorists it is widely debated whether we should rely on these models to evaluate humans' performance in judgment. Indeed, the existence of multiple models of rational attribution is due to the attempt of scholars to improve previous normative models. Thus, it seems that even within the field of attribution theory there is not full consensus regarding which normative criteria should be followed to make attributions.[178]

In addition, some of the normative standards of attribution that have been elaborated until now would not necessarily be considered criteria of good judgment in every situation in which individuals may find themselves.[179] Arguably this in the case for some normative theory of attribution in the context of trial settings. Some of the normative theories of attribution seem to be not well suited to serve as a criterion for evaluating judges' performance. For instance, Ross's criterion[180]

---

176 Levinson and Peng (2004). See also: Jeffrey Rachlinski, 2011. The Psychological Foundations of Behavioral Law and Economics. 201(5) U. ILL L. REV. 1675.

177 Giesen (2010).

178 Jennings (2010); For critiques moved to the normative theories of attribution illustrated above see for instance: Morris and Larrick (1995); Krueger Joachim and David Funder, 2004. Social Psychology: A Field in Search of a Center. 27(3) BEHAV. BRAIN SCI, 361.

179 Krueger and Funder (2004).

180 Ross (1977).

is a clear example of an ill-suited criterion. Despite Ross' argument has been dubbed attribution's theory fundamental rule of logic, it is not necessarily logical as the existence of an alternative sufficient situational cause cannot exclude that a disposition played a role in determining the observed behavior. For instance, in a car accident, the presence of a strong gust of wind that may have caused the accident (a sufficient situational cause) does not exclude the possibility that the driver was extremely tired (because he has a propensity to drive long hours without resting) and that the accident was caused by his behavior. As such, attribution theory's fundamental rule of logic would represent a questionable criterion to evaluate courts' performance.

Third, once identified whether the literature on the FAE poses a particular issue to be addressed, the policy responses to the problem depend, once again, on the normative criterion adopted. To illustrate, let's consider debiasing strategies. Above, I have discussed the use of accountability to reduce the effect of the FAE on courts' decisions. Nonetheless, the nature of the evidence provided by Tetlock's experiment grants limited support to the claim that human attributions could be made more accurate by making individuals accountable for their judgments. This is because this study interpreted the FAE from a coherence perspective.[181] In other words, Tetlock showed that accountability makes individuals less likely to infer dispositional traits from observed behaviors, but it did not deal with issues of correspondence.[182] Thus, it could be that these less dispositionally oriented judgments may not completely offset the effect of the FAE on subjects' attributions or, even worse, make the judgment even less accurate by overcorrecting it. This implies that legal scholars that support a correspondence theory of judicial truth should be cautious in suggesting debiasing strategies on the basis of studies that look at debiasing from a coherence perspective.

2.5 Conclusions

This Chapter has discussed the role of truth as a standard to evaluate human competence in making judgments and its use to assess the courts' performance at trial. Legal scholarship that applies behavioral insights to understand and predict courts' decisions translates judgment errors committed in experimental settings

181 Tetlock (1985).

182 Ibid.

into mistakes committed in trial settings. This scholarly practice, while potentially highly informative, can also lead to misleading findings when little attention is paid to differences in truth standards adopted in judgement and decision-making. The main contribution of this Chapter is to stress the importance of this issue for a scientifically sound development of behavioral law and economics. In particular, by focusing on the psychological literature on the FAE and its application to judicial decision-making, the Chapter highlights the following three issues related to the application of behavioral findings to trial settings to which legal scholarship may want to pay greater attention.

First, scholars that adopt coherence as the relevant criterion to evaluate trial performance, should be wary of blindly translating normative criteria adopted in JDM to assess the decision-making of judges. Indeed, as highlighted above, coherence criteria adopted in JDM are sometimes questionable. This applies, for instance to what I dubbed the "Ross' criterion"[183]. Second, depending on the normative criterion/a adopted to evaluate a legal system, JDM findings can or cannot highlight the existence of a problem. In this connection, the strength of the evidence supporting the existence of a problem is often strictly dependent on the criteria adopted. Third, also the set of policy responses available to address the identified problem and their desirability depend, once again, on the normative criterion adopted.

A failure to carefully consider these three issues when applying behavioral insights to the study of judicial decision-making may lead to undesirable consequences, such as: identification of inexistent problems; overestimation of the policy relevance of a problem; application of (maybe partially) ineffective or even counterproductive remedies to identified problems. To the extent that behavioral law and economics wants to be an empirically driven field of research that aspires to provide useful policy-relevant insights these are non-trivial issues to be considered.

This Chapter has discussed the relevance of these issues by making reference to studies on the FAE. It has highlighted how all the three types of problem discussed above apply to part of the legal literature on this behavioral phenomenon. It is not my contention that all the legal literature on the FAE suffers from these problems. Yet, it is clear that a substantial part does. In this regard, what is very

183 Ross (1977).

surprising is that even situationists, which ground their whole literature on in psychological studies on the FAE, pay little attention to these issues.

It is possible that other strands of literature within behavioral law and economics are less affected by these problems than the one specifically concerned with the FAE. As such, this Chapter should not be seen as a general critique to behavioral law and economics. Instead, it highlights some issues that, perhaps, are easily overlooked by legal scholars and call for more attention towards these problems.

More generally, by discussing the role of truth standards in JDM and judicial decision-making, this Chapter provides a general introduction to the study of the interplay between accuracy and behavioral law and economics that is relevant for understanding some of the arguments put forward in the remaining part of this book. In addition, the Chapter has also reviewed the legal literature on the FAE, which is also the starting point of the analysis for the following Chapter.

3 The Fundamental Attribution Error and Accuracy: Judges vs Jurors[184]

3.1 Introduction

As discussed in the previous Chapter, studies on the FAE had a prominent influence on tort law scholarship. Several authors have raised concerns that judges may systematically misattribute fault to the detriment of accuracy as well as lead to unwarranted developments of legal rules and practices. Despite this importance, existent empirical studies largely ignore whether expert adjudicators commit the FAE in trial settings. In particular, while psychological research indicates that the FAE is caused both by contextual factors and by individual tendencies of the adjudicator,[185] existing legal research has focused solely on the interplay of expertise and some type of contextual triggers of the FAE.[186] In addition, the few studies that have addressed this issue provide mixed results and focus on adjudicators with substantial experience.[187] This leaves uncertainty regarding whether, and under which conditions, individuals trained in law and adjudication are likely to fall prey to this error in legal settings.

The United States and European Civil law countries tend to adopt opposed strategies to minimize the risks of errors in the attribution of fault. European coun-

184 This Chapter is partially a reproduction of the following article: Goran Dominioni, Peter Desmet, and Louis Visscher, 2020, Judges Versus Jurors: Biased Attributions in the Courtroom, 52:1 CORNELL INTERNATIONAL LAW JOURNAL 102. I thank Maria Bigoni, Jeffrey Rachlinski, the participants to the 13th Conference on Empirical Legal Studies at Cornell Law School, to the IMPRS poster presentation at the Friedrich-Schiller-Universität Jena, to the BACT Lunch Seminar at Erasmus University Rotterdam, and the Italian Society of Law and Economics 12th Annual Conference for useful discussion. I am also very grateful to Sara Mahmoud for invaluable organizational support.

185 Gilbert and Malone (1995); Bauman Christopher and Linda Skitka, 2010. Making Attributions for Behaviors: The Prevalence of Correspondence Bias in the General Population. 32(3) BASIC APPL. SOC. PSYCHOL. 269.

186 See, for instance: Wallace Brian and Saul Kassin, 2012. Harmless Error Analysis: How Do Judges Respond to Confession Errors?, 36(2) LAW HUM. BEHAV. 155.

187 Wallace and Kassin (2012).

G. Dominioni, *Biased Trials*, Ökonomische Analyse des Rechts | Economic Analysis of Law, https://doi.org/10.1007/978-3-658-30080-7_3

tries employ almost exclusively judges for fact-finding, assuming that they perform well, and better than jurors, at this task.[188] The United States, instead, tend to rely more on the wisdom of the layperson (i.e. jurors) but adopt stricter evidentiary rules to limit the use of potentially biasing items of evidence.[189] A type of evidence that is particularly relevant in this regard, is the one that regulates the use of character evidence. Character evidence informs factfinders about past behaviors of one of the parties at trial. Many scholars consider character evidence a type of evidence that may lead judges and jurors to make faulty attributions at trial.[190] With some exceptions, US law insulates the jury from this type of evidence. European legal systems do not adopt this strict ban. Instead, they often dictate judges to assign the lowest probative value to character evidence.[191]

Despite the longstanding debate on which of these two systems produces better trial decisions,[192] their relative performance remains largely untested. Prominent legal scholars defend the idea that judges are less prone to commit the FAE at trial on the ground that experience in adjudication refines judges' ability to attribute responsibility,[193] and that individuals that embark in a judicial career are generally less prone to commit attributional errors than the general population.[194] But, is this so? This Chapter analyzes this question empirically.

---

188 Simona Grossi, 2010. A Comparative Analysis Between Italian Civil Proceedings and American Civil Proceedings Before Federal Courts, 20 IND. INT'L & COMP. L. REV., 213.

189 John Sheldon and Peter Murray, 2003. Rethinking the Rules of Evidentiary Admissibility in Non-Jury Trials. 86 JUDICATURE 227; Grossi (2010).

190 Frederick Vars, 2014. Behavioural Economics and Evidence Law, in THE OXFORD HANDBOOK OF BEHAVIORAL ECONOMICS AND THE LAW. Zamir, E., & Teichman, D. (Eds.) Oxford University Press. 703; see also Chris Sanchirico, 2001. Character Evidence and the Object of Trial. 101(6) COLUM. L. REV. 1227.

191 Michele Taruffo, 2012. La Prova nel Processo Civile, GIUFFRÉ EDITORE, 345 (2012). See also, Grossi (2010).

192 Sheldon and Murray, (2003); See also Frederick Schauer, 2006. On the Supposed Jury-Dependence of Evidence Law, 155(1) U. PA. L. REV 165 194. See also generally David A. Sklansky, 2009. Anti-Inquisitorialism, 122 HARV.L. REV. 1634.

193 Adam Benforado and Jon Hanson, 2008. The Great Attributional Divide: How Divergent Views of Human Behavior Are Shaping Legal Policy, 57 EMORY L.J., 311.

194 Benforado and Hanson, (2008). Relatedly, there is also a widespread belief among US judges and legal scholars that judges are better able than laypeople to ignore inadmissible items of evidence, such as character evidence. On legal scholarship, see, for instance, FED. JUDICIAL CTR., MANUAL FOR COMPLEX LITIGATION (Fourth) § 11.431, at 64 (2004); Leo Levin and Harold Cohen, 1971. The Exclusionary Rules in Nonjury Criminal Cases, 119 U. PA. L. REV. 905; An-

This Chapter is also the first to analyze whether continental Europe's regulation of character evidence is effective in reducing the risk that factfinders commit the FAE at trial. In doing so, it complements previous studies that focused on the effectiveness of American rules on inadmissible evidence in addressing errors in judicial decision-making,[195] thus allowing a comparison of the performance of the two systems.

I find that laypeople commit errors when applying European rules of character evidence. Since these rules aim to prevent errors in the attribution of responsibility, the results indicates that the European legal system is not able to prevent mistakes when fact-finding is performed by jurors. Thus in jury trials, American rules on the inadmissibility of character evidence seem a more appropriate choice. The results show also that judges are instead able to correctly apply European rules of character evidence and thus are more likely to avoid errors in fact-finding when character evidence is presented at trial. When taken together, these findings indicate that evidence rules in both the United States and Europe are well set up.

However, the results also indicate that neither of the two systems is able to prevent judges and jurors from committing errors in the attribution responsibility when these mistakes are not due to items of evidence presented at trial, such as character evidence, but to (unconscious) beliefs held by factfinders themselves. In particular, I find that the two groups have a similar propensity to commit the FAE; and that in both samples, those who have a (unconscious) personal tendency to commit the FAE consistently assign greater responsibility to tortfeasors. In particular, I find that judges and laypeople have a similar propensity to commit the FAE; and that in both groups participants that have a tendency to commit the FAE are more likely to hold the defendant responsible for the accident, regardless of

drew Wistrich et al., 2005. Can Judges Ignore Inadmissible Information? The Difficulty of Deliberately Disregarding. 153(4) U. PA. L. REV., 1251. On judicial opinions see Harris v. Rivera, 454 U.S. 339, 346 (1981); State v. Garcia, 397 P.2d 214, 216 (Ariz. 1964); Commonwealth v. Davis, 421 A.2d 179, 183 n.6 (Pa. 1980); Commonwealth v. Glover, 405 A.2d 945 (Pa. Super. Ct. 1979).

195 For a recent review of this literature see Doron Teichman and Eyal Zamir, 2014. Judicial Decision-Making A Behavioral Perspective, in The Oxford Handbook Of Behavioral Economics and The Law, (Zamir, E., & Teichman, D. Eds.) OXFORD UNIVERSITY PRESS, 664; Wistrich et al. (2015). For a review of psychological and sociological research on character evidence see generally Mike Redmayne, 2015. Character in The Criminal Trial, Oxford Monographs on Criminal and Justice, OXFORD UNIVERSITY PRESS.

whether character evidence is presented at trial. This result suggests that neither American nor European trials are likely to be bulletproof against the FAE.

This work unfolds as follows: Section 2 introduces the economic literature on evidence law and discusses character evidence and expertise in adjudication as determinants of the FAE. Section 3 describes the experiment. The results are reported in Section 4 and discussed in Section 5. Section 6 elaborates on the limitations of this study and Section 7 concludes.

3.2 Background Literature

3.2.1 A Short Introduction to the Economics of Evidence Law

Procedural rules of evidence regulate what type of information courts receive at trial and how this information should be used under different circumstances. From the perspective of law and economics this information flow and usage should be regulated to attain social welfare maximization.[196] In designing legal rules and practices that move towards this aim, economically minded scholars often assign an important role to accuracy in adjudication. As discussed above, it is widely believed that in a world in which the achievement of perfect accuracy is not costly, adjudication would attain social welfare maximization by pursuing accuracy at trial.[197] Yet, to the extent that obtaining perfect accuracy in adjudication is costly, one of the main aims of procedural law becomes the minimization of the social cost of errors in adjudication and their avoidance.[198] This optimal outcome is attained when the marginal benefit of an additional item of evidence equals the marginal cost of obtaining it.[199]

While theoretically intuitive, the achievement of social welfare maximization via procedural law finds three main obstacles in practice. First, the private and the public interest in accuracy in adjudication are not perfectly aligned.[200] While the collective aim is to maximize social welfare, private litigants maximize their own

196 Kaplow (2015).

197 Ibid.

198 Richard Posner, 2011. Economic Analysis of Law, 8th ed., ASPEN PUBLISHERS, 757.

199 Richard Posner, 1999. An Economic Approach to the Law of Evidence. Stanford Law Review, 1485; Alex Stein, 2015. The New Doctrinalism: Implications for Evidence Theory, 51(6) UNIV. PA. LAW REV 163.

200 Alex Stein, 2005. Foundations of Evidence Law, OXFORD UNIVERSITY PRESS.

utility (e.g. the expected value of litigation). Second, some of the information that is needed for accurate findings at trial is private or unavailable.[201] For instance, with regards to private information, a tortfeasor may know whether he was speeding at the moment of the accident, but this information might not be available to the court. In addition, whether a certain conduct (e.g. the release of pollution) has caused a certain harm (e.g. a cancer) might not be known by anyone. Given the diverging interests of trial parties and those of society, there is a risk that the former take advantage of courts' inability to observe information to pursue their private interests.[202] Third, when behavioral insights are taken into account, the information that parties provide to the court can influence courts' JDM in an unwarranted manner. For instance, in the case of the FAE, when informed about past accidents, courts may overestimate the degree by which a particular conduct was due to the dispositions of the tortfeasor, and thus overestimate the probability that the accident under scrutiny at trial was due to the negligent behavior of the driver. In order to minimize the costs of a miss-allocations of liability, legal systems rely on different types of evidence rules.

Law and economics has long studied remedies to the problems highlighted above. This strand of research suggests that legal systems can obviate these issues by regulating standards and burdens of proof, provide incentives to trial parties to provide truthful information, steer errors in the imposition of liability or limit/forbid the admission of information at trial.[203] As discussed above, behavioral law and economics has built upon and expanded the sets of remedies available by focusing on the interplay between the contextual environment in which adjudication takes place and human motivation/cognition. The next section further elaborates on this point with specific regard to the issue addressed in this Chapter.

3.2.2 The Fundamental Attribution Error: Contextual Determinants

Research in psychology has highlighted a multitude of triggers of the FAE.[204] These triggers can be located either in the person of the observer or in the situation

---

201 Ibid.

202 Ibid.

203 Ibid.

204 Gilbert and Malone (1995); Gawronski Bertram, 2003. Implicational Schemata and the Correspondence Bias: on the Diagnostic Value of Situationally Constrained Behavior. 84(6) J. PERS. SOC. PSYCHOL, 1154. Bauman and Skitka (2010).

surrounding her. On the situational side of the coin, existing scholarship often mentions character evidence as a main trigger of the FAE.[205] This type of evidence provides adjudicators with information about past behaviors of one of the parties at trial to be used to evaluate the epistemic status of the claims made by the plaintiff/defendant. Thus, for example, the victim of a car accident may present evidence regarding past car accidents caused by the defendant to prove her negligent behavior in the case at hand. However, the concern with the FAE is that the observer (i.e. the adjudicator) will overestimate the likelihood that the accident under scrutiny was caused by the negligent behavior of the target (the defendant) instead of, for instance, poor road conditions. Thus, the availability of character evidence may trigger the FAE.

In behavioral law and economics the possibility of committing the FAE is often cited as a major rationale underlying the existence of rules that aim to inhibit the misuse of character evidence.[206]

Under US law, the ban on character evidence is set forth by Federal Rule of Evidence (FRE) 404. This provision is part of a broader set of rules inspired by epistemic paternalism that regulates the admissibility of evidence at trial with the aim of preventing the jury from taking a decision on the basis of items of evidence whose "probative value is substantially outweighed by a danger of […] unfair prejudice, confusing the issues, misleading the jury".

Interestingly, the legislative ban on character evidence in US law is rarely mirrored by a similar rule in Continental Europe. As a consequence, Civil law judges are routinely exposed to a considerable amount of propensity evidence.[207] For instance, under Italian law,[208] with some exceptions, this type of evidence is freely admissible at trial. Yet, even in Europe the use of character evidence is not completely unregulated. In fact, while the principle of free evaluation of evidence is a core principle of evidentiary rules in many European countries, adjudicators

205 Vars (2014).

206 Vars (2014).

207 Mirjan Damaška, 1994. Propensity Evidence in Continental Legal Systems, 70 CHICAGO-KENT LAW REV. 65; Stewart Field, 2006. State, Citizen, and Character in French Criminal Process, 33(4) J. LAW SOC 522.

208 The present experiment was conducted with Italian subjects. For this reason, this section puts emphasis on the regulation of character evidence under Italian law. Yet, similar rules are found in other civil law systems (see on this: Damaška (1997)).

are expected to evaluate evidence according to rational standards.[209] In this connection, character evidence is often considered an item of evidence with the lowest probative value.[210] Therefore, legal scholars argue that adjudicators cannot hold the defendant liable when the only evidence available at trial is character evidence.[211] In this sense, European adjudicators are expected to not overestimate the probative value of this type of evidence. This expectation can be seen as an attempt by the legal system to avoid the influence of the FAE on judicial decisions. In the present work, I test the effectiveness of this (unwritten) rule to reduce the use of character evidence at trial. In doing so, I shed new light on whether rules that aim to reduce the influence of the FAE are effective in achieving their aim.

3.2.3 The Fundamental Attribution Error and Expert Adjudicators' Decision-Making

Besides contextual factors, such as character evidence, empirical research has also highlighted the existence of individual differences in the propensity to commit the FAE.[212] Adam Benforado and Jon Hanson[213] put forward the hypothesis that judges are less likely to commit the FAE than laypeople, at least in trial settings. While their claim is restricted to the American judiciary, the factors that they identify to support their conclusion are widely shared by European judiciaries. In fact, their claim is based on the following observations:

i) Judges are routinely confronted with the task of making attributions for human behavior.[214] This factor, in their view, should allow judges to test their consciously and unconsciously held beliefs on the determinants of human behavior (dispositions vs situational factors), and thus bring judges towards a view of the world that is more attentive to the power of situational factors.[215]

---

209 Taruffo (2014).

210 Damaška (1997); Simona Grossi and Maria Pagni, 2010. Commentary on the Italian Code of Civil Proceeding, OXFORD UNIVERSITY PRESS, 13.

211 Damaška (1997); Grossi and Pagni (2010).

212 Bauman and Skitka (2010).

213 Benforado and Hanson (2008).

214 Ibid.

215 Ibid.

ii) Judges, because of their role, are expected to make decisions that are fair, legitimate and well-reasoned.[216] This again may bring them to look more carefully at situational cues to make sense of the facts under scrutiny at trial.
iii) Judges' attention to situational factors might be enhanced by institutional mechanisms and procedures of the trial.[217] For instance, by debating in front of the court, trial parties may highlight various contextual factors that might have influenced the conduct under scrutiny.[218]
iv) Individuals that are more prone to understand the complex influence of situational factors on human behavior may self-select in the judiciary.[219] This, in turn, may create an environment in the judiciary that further promotes situationists views.[220]
v) Situationism in the judiciary is enhanced when adjudicators are provided with the time and support (e.g. law clerks) to make their decisions.[221] This support should help them to undergo a more thorough deliberation on the facts under scrutiny at trial.
vi) Adjudicators are routinely confronted with opposing views (those of the parties and other trial participants such as e.g. experts) on a subject matter.[222] This diversity of encounters may help judges to learn how to distinguish situational from personality-based determinants of human behavior. For, instance this may occur, when subjects with very different backgrounds act similarly in a certain situation, indicating that this behavior is common across individuals that find themselves in that situation.[223]
vii) The accountability mechanisms (appeal review, publication of the motivation, etc.) that surround the adjudication process foster situationists views by pushing judges to think more thoroughly when making a decision.[224]

---

216 Ibid.
217 Ibid.
218 Ibid.
219 Ibid.
220 Ibid.
221 Ibid.
222 Ibid.
223 Ibid.
224 Ibid.

The overall outcome of their analysis is that, at least in trial settings, adjudicators are likely to hold a relatively more situationist view of human behavior than the general population.[225] Yet, this hypothesis awaits being tested.

Note that the hypothesis proposed by Benforado and Hanson is not obvious. Empirical research casts doubt on the effectiveness of some of the mechanisms described above to promote situationism. For instance, while it is true that their role, as well as the institutional environment in which judges operate, should motivate them to make accurate decisions, the feedback they receive on their performance is often rather limited.[226] In addition, while it might be the case that individuals that tend to look for complex explanations for human behavior self-select in the judiciary, this is not the only relevant demographic variable. For instance, high-status people tend to explain life events more as a result of a person's disposition and reject restorative views of punishment, i.e. views that focus on criminals' rehabilitation, than low-status people.[227] Judges are a high-status group both in the United States and in continental Europe.

Generally, research indicates that judges are only sometimes better able than laypeople to avoid making biased trial decisions.[228] While there are some important exceptions to this trend,[229] judges' decisions are often influenced by their

225 Ibid.

226 Chris Guthrie et al., 2007. Blinking On the Bench: How Judges Decide Cases, 93 CORNELL L. REV. 1.

227 Michael Varnum, et al., 2012. Social Class Differences in N400 Indicate Differences in Spontaneous Trait Inference,141(3) J. EXP. PSYCHOL. GEN, 518, reviewing this literature that indicates social class differences in propensity to commit the FAE; Kraus Michael and Dacher Keltner, 2013. Social Class Rank, Essentialism, and Punitive Judgment, 105(2) J. PERS. SOC. PSYCHOL. 247.

228 See generally Teichman and Zamir (2014).

229 See, for instance, Jeffrey Rachlinski, et al., 2011. Probable Cause, Probability, and Hindsight. 8(1) J. EMPIRICAL LEGAL STUD. 72.

political beliefs,[230] identity,[231] emotions[232] and biases.[233] A first important question, therefore, remains whether judges are really less prone to make faulty attributions of responsibility at trial. This work aims to provide an answer to this question.

A second question that remains on the table, is whether judges outperform laypeople in applying rules that the legal system sets to reduce the influence of the FAE on their own decisions. As mentioned above, when it comes to character evidence, European legal systems adopt safeguards that are less strict against the FAE than those found in American evidence law. This institutional arrangement is often justified by the idea that judges are able to correctly handle character evidence.[234] In this view, widely held by judges[235] and scholars[236], judges are unbiased factfinders who are able to avoid cognitive errors arising from exposure to this type of evidence.

Yet, does expertise in adjudication improve the ability to assign character evidence its legally prescribed probative value? Existing research on similar types of evidence provides mixed results. A meta-analysis of studies conducted with laypeople indicates that evidence of prior convictions has some impact on laypeople's decisions in mock trials.[237] A similar result was obtained in a 2005 study conducted on 265 US judges by Andrew Wistrich and co-authors,[238] who tested the judges' propensity to use inadmissible evidence in a series of civil and criminal cases. In each case, judges in the treatment group were presented with various

230 Lee Epstein, et al., 2013. The Behavior of Federal Judges: A Theoretical and Empirical Study of Rational Choice, HARVARD UNIVERSITY PRESS 65.

231 Oren Gazal-Ayal and Raanan Sulitzeanu-Kenan, 2010. Let My People Go: Ethnic In-Group Bias in Judicial Decisions - Evidence from a Randomized Natural Experiment, 7(3) J. EMPIRICAL LEGAL STUD. 403.

232 Andrew Wistrich et al., 2014. Heart Versus Head: Do Judges Follow The Law Of Follow Their Feelings, 93 TEX. L. REV., 855.

233 Chris Guthrie et al., 2009. The "Hidden Judiciary": An Empirical Examination of Executive Branch Justice, 58 DUKE L.J. 1477.

234 Sheldon and Murray (2003).

235 Harris v. Rivera (1981); State v. Garcia (1964); Commonwealth v. Davis (1980); Commonwealth v. Glover (1979).

236 See Fed. Judicial Ctr. (2004); Levin and Cohen (1971); Grossi (2010).

237 For a meta-analysis of this literature see: Devine Dennis and David Caughlin, 2014. Do They Matter? A Meta-Analytic Investigation of Individual Characteristics and Guilt Judgments, 20 (2) PSYCHOL. PUBLIC POLICY LAW 109.

238 Wistrich et al. (2005).

forms of inadmissible evidence. Of particular relevance for the present work are the third[239] and fourth[240] study, which analyzed the effect of parties' previous conducts (tendency to sexual promiscuity and previous convictions) on trial outcomes. These studies find that judges are not able to disregard this information.[241] This holds regardless of the years of experience of the judge.[242] While certainly informative, the study by Wistrich and co-authors does not fully capture the dynamics underlying the functioning of the FAE in relation to character evidence. In presence of character evidence, the FAE may lead individuals to overestimate the probability that a person's conduct will be repeated in the future. For this reason, it is important that the previous conduct (presented with the evidence) matches the one under scrutiny at trial. In the study conducted by Wistrich and co-authors,[243] previous criminal convictions for fraud are introduced in a tort trial to undermine the credibility of the plaintiff;[244] and in the sexual promiscuity evidence scenario, this evidence was provided to hint at the fact that the woman that was allegedly raped had in fact given her consent to the alleged rapist. Thus, in both scenarios, the evidence of the previous conduct was only partially related to the one under scrutiny at trial. My study differs from the one by Wistrich and co-authors in two main ways. First, I test the effect of previous convictions on the decisions made in a case that presents very similar facts. This is the most suitable way to test the FAE in relation to character evidence. Second, I test the European rule on character evidence, which contrary to American law, does not require to ignore character evidence, but only to assign it the lowest probative value.

Another strand of literature that is relevant for the present study is the one that, more generally, analyses judges' ability to disregard inadmissible information.[245] Landsman and Rakos test in a tort law scenario whether judges and lay adjudicators differ in their ability to disregard evidence of subsequent remedial measures. This study found no differences between the two groups.[246] Similar

239 Ibid.

240 Ibid.

241 Ibid.

242 Ibid.

243 Ibid.

244 Ibid.

245 Teichman and Zamir (2014).

246 Stephan Landsman and Richard Rakos, 1994. A Preliminary Inquiry into the Effect of Potentially Biasing Information on Judges and Jurors in Civil Litigation, 12(2) BEHAV. SCI. & L., 113.

findings were obtained in a more recent work by Saul Wallace and Holly Kassin.[247] Here judges were not able to disregard information obtained with coercion during an interrogation. Again, this result was not dependent on judges' experience. This study replicated with judges a result that was obtained in an early analysis conducted with laypeople.[248] When taken together, this research suggests that the two groups (judges and laypeople) were similarly prone to use inadmissible evidence.

Against these findings, Chris Guthrie and co-authors find evidence that American administrative judges are able to ignore improperly authenticated evidence in a hypothetical trial scenario.[249] Similarly, a recent study shows that judges, regardless of years of experience at the bench, make similar decisions in hindsight and foresight when establishing probable cause.[250] This suggests that judges are not unduly influenced by the hindsight information. Overall, research on the effect of inadmissible evidence on experts' decision-making indicates that judges are sometimes able to provide inadmissible evidence its due probative value. Yet, given the mixed findings of this literature, it is difficult to predict under which conditions this occurs.

In this Chapter, I complement this literature by studying whether participants in the experiment are able to correctly apply rules of evidence adopted by several European legal systems to reduce the risk of errors in the attribution of responsibility at trial. In particular, I focus on evidentiary rules prevailing in Italy, but that are common to other main Civil law traditions.[251] In doing so, I set the basis for an empirically informed debate on the relative performance of the American and the European legal systems.

---

247 Brian Wallace Saul Kassin, 2012. Harmless Error Analysis: How Do Judges Respond To Confession Errors?, 36(2) LAW & HUM. BEHAV. 151.

248 Saul Kassin and Holly Sukel, 1997. Coerced Confessions and the Jury: An Experimental Test of the "Harmless Error" Rule. 21(1) LAW & HUM. BEHAV. 27.

249 Guthrie et al. (2009).

250 Rachlinski et al. (2011).

251 Damaška (1994); Field (2006).

3.3 The Experiment

3.3.1 Participants

Most of the existing studies on expertise in adjudication have been conducted with judges that had on average substantial (i.e. more than 10 years) of experience serving at the bench.[252] In addition, studies on expertise and decision-making often compare experts with subjects that have no experience whatsoever in performing tasks tested in the experiment.[253] Comparing senior experts with individuals that have no experience in performing adjudication tasks is certainly a meaningful enterprise to spot differences among the two groups. However, this clear-cut distinction captures only one part of reality. Nowadays most Western legal systems employ a large number of non-professional judges that serve the bench for very limited periods of time and that often have broad jurisdiction in civil and criminal cases.

The selection criteria and appointment status vary from legal system to legal system as well as across different sub-categories of non-professional judges. For example, in Italy, more than 3700 honorary judges (vis-a-vis 6485 professional judges) routinely carry out judicial activities both in criminal and civil law trials. Italian honorary judges are nominated for a limited period of time (three or four years, renewable only once) and are chosen among individuals that have some degree of familiarity with the law (depending on the type of honorary judge either a standard law degree or having passed the bar exam).[254]

Similarly, non-professional judges play a major role in the justice system of several EU countries.[255] In addition, the use of non-professional judges is not confined only to the European experience. For instance, US justice courts employ a large number of non-professional judges with functions that vary from state to

---

252 Wistrich et al. (2005); Guthrie et al. (2009); Rachlinski et al. (2011); Wallace and Kassin (2012).

253 Ian Belton et al, 2014. Lawyer and Nonlawyer Susceptibility to Framing Effects in Out-of-Court Civil Litigation Settlement. 11(3) J. EMPIRICAL LEGAL STUD 578.

254 Silvia Ciotti Galetti, 2004. The Italian Court Honorary Judges, in Policing in Central and Eastern Europe, in DILEMMAS OF CONTEMPORARY CRIMINAL JUSTICE, 443, 444 (Gorazd Meško, Milan Pagon, Bojan Dobovšek eds.).

255 See generally Eric Dubois, Christel Schurrer, Marco Velicogna The Functioning of Judicial Systems and the Situation of the Economy in the European Union Member States, 2013. REPORT PREPARED FOR THE EUROPEAN COMMISSION (DIRECTORATE GENERAL JUSTICE), reviewing the use of non-professional judges in various European countries.

state.[256] In this connection, it can be interesting to expand the inquiry of the influence of cognitive errors in adjudication to samples of subjects that have only a limited experience in adjudication, as this can shed new light on the decision-making of judges that have served only for a relatively short period of time (e.g. judges in their early career and non-professional judges).

To fill this gap, I recruited two independent samples of subjects. The first was composed of 100 individuals (male = 35%; average age = 25.9; SD = 1.22) enrolled in a Scuola di Specializzazione per le Professioni Legali (SSPL). SSPLs are two-year post JD schools that prepare law graduates to become Italian magistrates. 60 of the SSPL participants were enrolled in the second year of the SSPL, while the remaining were enrolled in the first year. I collected data on first year and second year SSPL participants on two different days. I am therefore able to distinguish the answers provided by the two groups. Attendance to a SSPL provides direct access to the competitive public exam to access the judicial career. Nowadays, SSPLs are the main route via which magistrates are recruited in Italy.[257] Participation was incentivized through the offer of a buffet and a lottery with a 100 euro prize (about 117 USD).

To make sure that subjects in the sample were attending the school to subsequently join the judiciary, I asked participants after completion of the experiment whether they intended to enter the judiciary. Out of the 100 participants, 94 replied that they desire to enter the judiciary after the completion of the school. This sample is therefore composed of subjects that are very close to complete the education necessary to access the exam to enter the Italian judiciary and that, at the time of

---

256 See, for instance, the employment of justices in New York that do not have a law degree: Susan Patnode, Julie Davies, Lisa Frisch, 2017. Behind the Scenery, A Rural New York Portrait, in Rural Justice in New York State: Challenges and Recommendations, 17 GOV'T, L. & POL'Y J. 1, 6. Note also that many professional judges in the US have little prior experience in practising law. For instance, in 2014, 45.4% of had no such U.S. circuit court judges had no prior experience as a judge before their appointment to a circuit court. Among those that had no prior experience as judges, about 20% had no experience as lawyers in private practice, see on this Barry McMillion, 2014. U.S. Circuit Court Judges: Profile of Professional Experiences Prior to Appointment, CRS REPORT, 1.

257 Giuseppe Di Federico, 2005. Recruitment, Professional Evaluation, Career and Discipline of Judges and Prosecutors in Italy, in RECRUITMENT, PROFESSIONAL EVALUATION AND CAREER OF JUDGES AND PROSECUTORS IN EUROPE. ISTITUTO DI RICERCA SUI SISTEMI GIUDIZIARI, Giuseppe (Di Federico Eds.) 1, 128.

the experiment, were to a large extent still motivated to pursue the judicial career. For this reason, I refer to them as to "judges-to-be".

The second group was composed of 129 university students (male = 32,56%; average age = 21,2; SD = 2.28) enrolled in a law school (both at the graduate and undergraduate level, as Italian law schools are not divided into bachelor and master). No incentive was provided for participation. They were recruited in university libraries of the same city in which the SSPL is located. Subjects were selected with these criteria to provide some basic control for educational background and geographical location.

I compare the decision-making of judges-to-be with that of law students to test the hypothesis put forward by Benforado and Hanson.[258] If it is the case that individuals that decide to enter the judiciary tend on average to be more situationist than the rest of the population, we can expect subjects that (after law school) embark on a judicial career to be less dispositionist (i.e. tend less to commit the FAE), than the average law student. This is for two reasons: i) there is no reason to believe that the average law student should be less situationist than the general population, thus a comparison with law students also provides information about the comparison with the general population; ii) unless one believes that lawyers, in general, are a category that sparks situationism in society as much as lawyers that aim to enter in the judiciary, we should observe a certain degree of self-selection among law students. For this reason, a meaningful comparison can be made between post-JDs that self-select in a judicial career and other law students.

I controlled whether the samples differed in terms of age and gender composition. I found no differences in terms of gender, and (not surprisingly) I found that judges-to-be were significantly older than law students. Note that the major difference between the educational curricula at a law school and an SSPL is that the former has an almost exclusive focus on learning positive law and legal reasoning. Conversely, the SSPL training has a stronger practical focus, which integrates theoretical learning with internships in courts and various practical courses (case law reading and drafting; legal counselling, mock trials, etc.).

---

[258] Benforado and Hanson (2008).

3.3.2 Design

I used a 2 × 2 quasi-experimental design. The independent variables were participant type (judges-to-be or law students) and character evidence (character evidence vs. non-character evidence). Respondents in each group were randomly assigned to one of the conditions (character evidence vs. non-character evidence).

3.3.3 Stimuli and Measures

All respondents were given a questionnaire divided into two parts. In the first part, I tested participants' personal tendencies to commit the FAE. To do so, I used the standard questionnaire on implicit theories of moral character.[259]

Research indicates that a predictor of individual variations in the tendency to commit this error are implicit (or lay) theories.[260] Lay theories are not scientific theories nor are they necessarily consciously held. Yet, individuals often use them in an unconscious way to understand their own behavior and that of others.[261] Implicit theories are categorized as tending either more towards situationism or to dispositionism.[262] The more the implicit theory is situationist, the more it tends to explain human behavior in terms of situational, contextual factors. Conversely, the less it is situationist (i.e. the more it is dispositionist), the more it stresses the role of personality. Individuals holding a dispositionist lay theory are more inclined to commit the FAE than people adhering to situationist beliefs. [263]

Within the lay theories strand of research, studies on implicit theories of moral character are particularly relevant for the study of attributions in trial settings.[264] Based on implicit theories of moral character, individuals can be categorized as either entity theorists or incremental theorists. Entity theorists have a rel-

---

259 Carol Dweck, 1995. Implicit Theories and Their Role in Judgments and Reactions: A Word from Two Perspectives, 6(4) PSYCHOL. INQ., 267.

260 Choi et al. (1999); Bauman and Skitka (2010). Carol Dweck, Implicit Theories, in HANDBOOK OF THEORIES OF SOCIAL PSYCHOLOGY (Vol 2, Paul A. M. Van Lange, Arie W. Kruglanski & E. Tory Higgins Eds.), SAGE Publications Ltd, 2, 52 (2012).

261 Dweck et al. (1995).

262 Ibid.

263 Choi et al. (1999); Bauman and Skitka (2010); Dweck (2012).

264 Chiu Chi-yue et al., 1997. Implicit Theories and Conceptions of Morality, 73(5) PERS. SOC. PSYCHOL., 923.

atively higher propensity to believe that moral traits are non-malleable. Entity theorists are therefore more prone to commit the FAE than incremental theorists.[265] In mock trials, for example, adherence to an entity theory of moral character has shown to predict a higher use of character evidence to establish guilt.[266] In a similar vein, Tam and co-authors found that entity theorists tend to hold stronger beliefs in criminal recidivism, dispositionally driven crime, and, as a result, impose higher punishments.[267] Furthermore, Tam and co-authors also found that higher punishments imposed by entity theorists were mediated by dispositionally oriented attributions.[268]

The questionnaire on implicit theories of moral character was translated into Italian with the help of a professional translator. The questionnaire is composed by the following three items: "A person's moral character is something very basic about them, and it can't be changed much"; 2) "Whether a person is responsible or sincere or not is deeply ingrained in their personality. It cannot be changed very much."; 3) "There is not much that can be done to change a person's moral traits (e.g. conscientiousness, uprightness and honesty)". Subjects were requested to express their agreement with each of the three statements on a 1 to 6 points scale and the answers were then combined in a scale to form a measure of implicit beliefs of moral character. The higher the score on this scale the more the respondent can be seen as an entity theorist (i.e. has a higher tendency to commit the FAE). I observe that the scale had an excellent internal consistency (Cronbach's $\alpha = .84$).

In the second part of the questionnaire, which contained the character evidence vs. non-character evidence treatment, respondents read a hypothetical tort law case in which a self-employed bricklayer was asked by a client to repair the roof of his house. 12 years after the reparation took place, a violent whirlwind hit the roof, hereby damaging it. The client sued the bricklayer arguing that the damage would not have occurred had the bricklayer used due care to repair the roof. The bricklayer, however, denied not having taken due care. It was explained that evidence at trial showed that it was more than 100 years ago that a whirlwind hit

---

265 David Silveran et al., 2000. The Association Between Implicit Theories of Personality and the Attribution Process, 41 SCAND. J PSYCHOL., 107; Dweck, supra note 97, at 52.

266 Benjamin Gervey et al., 1999. Differential Use of Person Information in Decisions about Guilt Versus Innocence: The Role of Implicit Theories, 25(1) PERS. SOC. PSYCHOL. BULL., 17;

267 Kim-Pong Tam et al., 2013. Belief about Immutability of Moral Characters and Punitiveness Toward Criminal Offenders, 43 J. APPL. SOC. PSYCHOL., 603.

268 Ibid.

that area. In addition, the expert report established that it is possible for a badly repaired roof to last 12 years, but the expert was not able to establish whether the bricklayer exercised due care when repairing the roof. Important to note is that the strong and unforeseeable whirlwind was mentioned in the scenario to introduce a situational factor that could explain the accident. Respondents in the character evidence condition, in addition, received the information that on two previous occasions the bricklayer was found liable for having negligently repaired a roof. On both occasions, the bricklayer was said to have denied responsibility and to have shown little consideration for the loss of his clients. This is the typical situation in which, under Italian law, judges are expected to ignore character evidence. In fact, given the low probative value attached to items of character evidence and the absence of other items of evidence against the plaintiff, the judge is expected to ignore this evidence.[269] Participants in the no character evidence condition did not receive the information.

Thus, the second part of the questionnaire tests whether subjects are able to provide character evidence its legally prescribed probative value and therefore correctly apply evidence rules that aim to limit attributional errors at trial. Note that given the specific features of this case, respondents have a relatively simple rule to follow (i.e. ignore character evidence). Thus, if they fail to correctly apply this rule in this occasion, it is plausible that they would not follow it in situations where the rule is less clear-cut. For instance, when they are called to give some weight to the item of evidence presented.

The dependent variables in each condition were the following: 1) I assessed respondents' attribution of the incident to situation vs. person by asking them to identify the cause/s of the accident on a 1-7 points scale (1 the sole cause of the accident was the violent whirlwind – 7 the sole cause of the accident was the conduct of the bricklayer); 2) participants were asked to imagine that they were judges presiding a case and to assign responsibility to the bricklayer for the accident. The answer had to be given on a 1-7 points scale (1 the bricklayer is not responsible at all - 7 the bricklayer is fully responsible). This is the key dependent variable that tests the attribution of legal responsibility to the defendant; 3) I concluded the questionnaire by asking participants which percentage of the damages had to be compensated by the bricklayer.

269 Grossi (2010).

I expected that respondents who received character evidence attribute more causality and responsibility to the plaintiff and require him to compensate a larger percentage of the harm compared to subjects that did not receive character evidence. Given the mixed findings of previous research on the relative performance of judges and laypeople in using inadmissible information,[270] I expect judges-to-be to be less affected by character evidence than law students. Building on previous research on implicit theories of moral character and trial decisions,[271] I expect that respondents' score on the implicit theories dimension predicts the attribution of causality, responsibility and damages awards.

3.4 Results

Before testing the hypotheses, following the procedure described by Dweck and co-authors I compute the proportion of entity and incremental theorists in both samples.[272] I find that respectively 48% and 49% of the judges-to-be and law students are incremental theorists. This finding is in line with the general results according to which approximately 50% of the American participants are classified as incremental theorists.[273] This indicates that judges-to-be have the same propensity to commit the FAE as participants of previous studies conducted in the United States. In line with previous literature on implicit theories, the remainder of the analysis used the implicit theories of moral character as a scale variable.[274]

General Linear Models were used to estimate the effect of the independent variables (participant type; character evidence, implicit theories) on the dependent variables.

3.4.1 Manipulation check

To verify whether the manipulation was successful, I asked participants on a 7-point Likert scale to what degree they believed that the defendant had a history of not repairing roofs properly (1 not at all - 7 very much). A General Linear Model with both the manipulation (character evidence and training), standardized scores

270 Teichman and Zamir (2014).

271 Gervey et al. (1999); Tam et al. (2013).

272 Dweck, et al. (1995).

273 Silveran et al. (2000).

274 Dweck et al. (1995).

on the implicit theories scale and their interaction as predictors revealed only a main effect for treatment, $F(1, 222) = 172.50$, $p < .001$, $\eta^2 = .44$, indicating that participants in the character evidence condition (M = 5.14, SD = 1.38) were more inclined to believe that the defendant had a history of not repairing roofs properly than participants in the no character evidence condition (M = 2.65, SD = 1.49). This indicated the manipulation was successful.

3.4.2 Attribution of causality

The same analysis as for the manipulation check was conducted for the dependent variable attribution of causality. Results revealed a main effect for character evidence, $F(1, 222) = 8.27$, $p < .005$, $\eta 2 = .04$, indicating that participants in the character evidence condition (M = 3.10, SD = 1.16) were more inclined to attribute the incident to the defendant's conduct (or less inclined to attribute to the situation) than participants in the no character evidence condition (M = 2.63, SD = 1.15). This analysis also reveals a significant main effect of type of participant, $F(1, 222) = 8.15$, $p = .005$, $\eta 2 = .04$, indicating that law students (M = 3.05, SD = 1.17) were more inclined to attribute the incident to the defendant's conduct (or less inclined to attribute to the situation) than judges-to-be (M = 2.61, SD = 1.14). The analysis revealed no other effects, except for a marginally significant main effect of implicit theories, $F(1, 222) = 2.67$, $p = .10$, $\eta 2 = .01$, indicating that the more participants are dispositionally inclined to attribute to dispositions, the more they did attribute the accident to the defendant's conduct. This effect, as well as the one relative to character evidence, did not differ between first and second year judges-to be.

Table 1 Mean Response (Causality, Responsibility and Damages Award) by Condition and Total

Evidence Type	Judges-To-Be				Law Students		
	Character	Non-Character	Total		Character	Non-Character	Total
Causality	2.82	2.41	2,61		3.34	2.80	3,06
Responsibility	2.57	2.27	2,42		3.48	2.64	3,06
Damages Award	21.94	18.24	20,05		32.54	22.89	27,32

3.4.3 Responsibility

I repeated the analysis for the responsibility variable and observed a main effect for character evidence, $F(1, 222) = 9.07$, $p < .005$, $\eta^2 = .04$, suggesting that subjects in the character evidence condition ($M = 3.08$, $SD = 1.45$) had a tendency to judge the defendant to be more responsible than participants in the non-character evidence condition ($M = 2.48$, $SD = 1.32$). The analysis also shows a significant main effect of type of participant, $F(1, 222) = 12.00$, $p = .001$, $\eta^2 = .05$, suggesting that judges-to-be ($M = 2.42$, $SD = 1.34$) were less inclined to assign responsibility to the defendant than law students ($M = 3.05$, $SD = 1.42$). These main effects were, however, qualified by a marginally significant interaction, $F(1, 222) = 2.69$, $p = .10$, $\eta^2 = .01$. Closer inspection (Pairwise comparisons with Bonferroni adjustments) showed that whereas law students receiving character evidence did assign more responsibility ($M = 3.45$, $SD = 1.35$) than law students who did not receive character evidence ($M = 2.64$, $SD = 1.37$), for judges-to-be this was not the case: respondents who received character evidence did not assign significantly more responsibility to the defendant ($M = 2.57$, $SD = 1.43$) than respondents who did not receive character evidence ($M = 2.42$, $SD = 1.33$). I also find a significant, yet marginal, main effect of implicit theories, $F\ (1, 222) = 3.36$, $p < .10$, $\eta^2 = .01$, indicating the existence of a positive correlation between dispositionism and the attribution of responsibility. As above, a more fine-grained analysis showed that the effect of character evidence and implicit theories was not different between the first and second year judges-to-be.

3.4.4 Percentage of Damages Awarded

Lastly, the same analysis was conducted with the percentage of damages awarded as the dependent variable. Since a finding of responsibility is a precondition for requiring the defendant to compensate losses, I excluded from the sample the subjects that did not assign responsibility to the defendant. The analysis shows no significant main effect of treatment. In addition, the analysis also reveals the absence of a significant main effect of implicit theories.

3.5 Discussion

Are judges less prone to commit the FAE in trial settings than laypeople? Since both the type of evidence presented at trial and personal inclinations can trigger the FAE, answering this question requires looking at each of these factors.

First, the data show that judges-to-be score similarly to law students on the implicit theories of moral character. Therefore, the hypothesis put forward by Benforado and Hanson,[275] according to which people that embark on a judicial career tend to be more situationist than the rest of the population, is not supported by the data. Second, I find that for both groups (law students and judges-to-be) higher adherence to dispositionism is (marginally) associated with higher attribution of causality and responsibility to the plaintiff. In this connection, when read in conjunction with the studies on implicit theories, FAE and punishment,[276] the result suggests that in the present study entity theorists may have attributed higher responsibility and damages because of a failure to correct their dispositional inferences for situational factors.

This result is consistent with previous studies which find that, like laypeople, judges rely on cognitive processes that trigger the FAE. For instance, American and Dutch judges have been found to rely on anchoring and adjustment,[277] which is one of the mental processes that give rise to the FAE.[278] Feldman and co-authors find similar results with law students and experienced lawyers.[279] My findings thus suggest that neither the training received by judges-to-be nor self-selection in the profession shields them fully from committing attributional errors in trial settings.

In relation to the effect of character evidence on trial outcomes the results show that, contrary to law students, judges-to-be were better able to correctly apply the rule that limits the probative value of character evidence when expected to do so. This result holds true for the responsibility variable, but not for the causality one. This difference in results can be explained by the fact that, under Italian law, attributing fault is a legal endeavour, while establishing causality is not necessarily

275 Benforado and Hanson (2008).

276 Tam et al. (2013).

277 Jeffrey Rachlinski et al., 2015. Can Judges Make Reliable Numeric Judgments: Distorted Damages and Skewed Sentences, 90 IND. L.J., 695, 730-731;

278 Richard Nisbett and Lee Ross, 1980. Human Inference: Strategies and Shortcomings of Social Judgment, PRENTICE-HALL, 123.

279 Yuval Feldman et al., 2016. Anchoring Legal Standards. 13 J. EMPIRICAL LEGAL STUD., 298.

so. To explain, the Italian legal system, as many other systems, distinguishes the notion of causality, i.e. the factual relation between two events, from the one of causation, i.e. a legal concept subject to various rules, such as the requirement that a factor is a "necessary" cause of an accident.[280] My questionnaire asked participants to determine causality, not causation. Also, in the questionnaire, I stressed the legal relevance of the responsibility question by asking participants to imagine that they were judges presiding over a case. This framing was instead not present in the causality question. In line with previous research,[281] this finding suggests that judges-to-be perform better than law students when making legal decisions, but not when they are merely asked to attribute causality for events.

The result is consistent with the literature on the effect of character evidence on lay adjudicators, which shows that laypeople's trial decisions are affected by knowledge of prior convictions.[282] In addition, this result is also consistent with the evidence indicating that American administrative law judges are able to disregard inadmissible information.[283] Similarly, this study is in line with the recent finding by Rachlinski and co-authors that judges, regardless of years of experience in adjudication, are able to disregard hindsight information when expected to do so.[284] The results suggest that the employment of judges may reduce the influence of the FAE on trial outcomes, at least when this error is due to character evidence. What can explain this result? Given that I found no differences in terms of implicit theories among the two groups, which excludes self-selection as an explanation, it is plausible that the results were due to differences in familiarity with handling cases at trial between law students and judges-to-be. Indeed, it is plausible that, given their greater experience, judges-to-be perform better than law students in correctly applying rules limiting the probative value of character evidence.[285]

These results are surprising. Indeed, they are somewhat difficult to reconcile with part of the previous literature that finds that even professional judges with many years of professional experience are not always able to handle inadmissible

280 For a review see Infantino Marta and Eleni Zervogianni, 2017. The European Ways to Causation, in Causation in European Tort Law (Marta Infantino & Eleni Zervogianni. eds.) 94-95 CAMBRIDGE UNIVERSITY PRESS.

281 Rachlinski et al. (2011).

282 Devine and Caughlin (2014)

283 Guthrie et al. (2009).

284 Rachlinski et al. (2011).

285 On the role of experience in improving judicial decision-making see: Guthrie et al. (2009).

evidence as expected.[286] Yet, a common finding in this literature is that, when it comes to ignoring inadmissible evidence, the years of experience in the judiciary are irrelevant in predicting performance.[287] It can, therefore, be the case that there are *types* of evidence that are easy to ignore after having received little training in adjudication; while others are very difficult to ignore, regardless of experience. Yet, on the basis of current data, it is difficult to identify which types of character evidence are more easily ignored. Further research is needed in this direction. If little expertise is sufficient to ignore some type of character evidence but not others, one could conceive tailoring evidence law on the specific type of evidence considered.

My findings contribute to the transatlantic debate on the relative advantages of American evidence law and continental Europe evidence law in improving the accuracy of trial decisions. In particular, they indicate that even a softer regulation of character evidence than the one adopted under American law may sometimes be effective in steering adjudicators' decisions in the right direction. In particular, as discussed above, Italian law does not forbid the use of character evidence tout-court, but it requires the judge to ignore it when it is the only item of evidence available. Judges-to-be have shown to be able to act upon this prescription, at least when assigning responsibility. Overall, these findings offer some support to the idea, often held in legal scholarship, that a ban on character evidence might not always be necessary in legal systems that employ judges.[288] Thus, the institutional set-up put forward by legal systems on the two sides of the Atlantic seem to be well calibrated.[289] The almost exclusive employment of (professional and non-professional) judges in European countries may justify soft regulation of character evidence, but similar rules may not be warranted when decisions are made by jurors.

286 Wistrich et al. (2005); Wallace and Kassin (2012).

287 Wistrich et al. (2005); Rachlinski et al. (2011); Wallace and Kassin, (2012).

288 See Fed. Judicial Ctr., (2004); Levin and Cohen (1971); Sheldon and Murray (2003).

289 Note that European countries may gain from admitting character evidence at trial because this type of evidence can have some probative value. Thus, if well used, it can improve the accuracy of trial decision.

3.6 Limitations

Despite my efforts, the present work has various limitations. A first limit, common to all vignette experiments, is that subjects gave the behavioral responses in a hypothetical scenario. This methodology does not replicate the emotional and institutional incentives that factfinders receive in real life settings, and therefore the results have only a limited external validity. Yet, isolating the effects of the FAE on judicial decision-making is already a challenging task in artificial settings. Studying this phenomenon in the field would be even more difficult.

Second, subjects in this experiment were law students and judges-to-be that were approached in the same city. Despite the fact that the two groups are similar on many levels, and different for training received and professional aspirations, it is possible that the result was driven by another demographic factor. In this connection, a clear difference between the two samples was age. In line with academic practice, I controlled the results for age. The results were replicated. I controlled the results also for gender and obtained results in line with the previous ones.

3.7 Conclusion

Attributing fault is a key but challenging aspect of tort trials. A wealth of psychological research shows that humans are prone to make systematic errors in performing this task. Is there a remedy to this problem? The United States and continental Europe legal systems adopt diametrically opposed remedies to address this issue. European legal systems rely almost exclusively on judges to perform fact-finding, assuming that they make fewer mistakes than laypeople in attributing responsibility at trial. Under American law, instead, fact-finding is delegated to jurors, but some types of evidence are made inadmissible in trials to protect jurors from potentially biasing information, such as character evidence. Legal scholars debate on which of these two systems is better at reducing errors in fact-finding.

In this Chapter, I provide empirical evidence on the relative performance of these two systems via a vignette study. My findings indicate that, while the European approach to character evidence is not effective in preventing laypeople (i.e. jurors) from committing errors in the attribution of responsibility at trial, European rules are effective when fact-finding is performed by judges. Therefore, the American evidence law approach to limit the admissibility of character evidence at trial seems appropriate when fact-finding is performed by jurors. However, the results also indicate that neither of the two approaches can fully prevent factfinders' errors in attributing responsibility. In particular, I find that when these errors are due to unconscious beliefs held by factfinders, both judges and jurors' decisions reflect the propensity of the factfinder to commit errors at trial.

4 Implicit Racial Biases in Tort Trials[290]

4.1 Introduction

The previous two Chapters have focused on the FAE, which is psychological phenomena that had a large influence on tort law and evidence law scholarship. In particular, Chapter 2, has discussed some issues related to the misuse of psychological literature on the FAE to identify problems and policy responses to these problems in tort and criminal trials. Chapter 3 has provided an empirical analysis of the effect of the FAE on expert adjudicators' decisions at trial. This Chapter expands the scope of the behavioral analysis by studying other psychological phenomena that, like the FAE, relates to ingroup-outgroup membership and that have recently received growing attention in behavioral law and economics, i.e. implicit racial biases (IRBs). IRBs are biases driven by automatic and/or unconscious attitudes and stereotypes that individuals hold towards a particular social group identified by race.[291] So far, IRBs have been studied mostly in the context of the economics of criminal law.[292] The existing research has resulted in a prolific debate on the effects of, and the adequate

---

290 This Chapter is partially partially a reproduction of the encyclopedia entry: Dominioni Goran and Alessandro Romano, 2017. Trial (Implicit Biases), The Encyclopaedia of Law and Economics, SPRINGER; and it is based on the unpublished manuscript Dominioni Goran and Louis Visscher, Implicit Biases in Tort Trials, UNPUBLISHED MANUSCRIPT. I am grateful to Pieter Desmet, Christoph Engel, Alexandre Biard and Alessandro Romano, as well as to the participants at the 20th Ius Commune Conference at Leuven University, the BACT Lunch Seminar at Erasmus University of Rotterdam, the Future of Law and Economics Conference at Erasmus University of Rotterdam, the European Association of Psychology and Law 26th Annual Conference at Toulouse University and the IAREP/SABE 2016 Conference at Wageningen University for valuable feedback on earlier versions of this Chapter.

291 Jerry Kang et al., 2012. Implicit Bias in the Courtroom, 59 UCLA L. REV 1129. For more literature on IRBs, see among others Greenwald G. (2006), Implicit Bias: Scientific Foundations, 94(4) CAL. L. REV, 950; Gawronski Bertram and Keith Payne, 2012. A History of Implicit Social Cognition: Where Is It Coming From? Where Is It Now? Where Is It Going?, in Handbook of Implicit Social Cognition: Measurement, Theory, and Applications, (B.K. Payne and B. Gawronski Eds.), GUILFORD PRESS.

292 For a recent review of this literature see: Dominioni Goran and Alessandro Romano, 2017. Trial (Implicit Biases), Encyclopaedia of Law and Economics, SPRINGER.

G. Dominioni, *Biased Trials*, Ökonomische Analyse des Rechts | Economic Analysis of Law, https://doi.org/10.1007/978-3-658-30080-7_4

responses to, IRBs.[293] In this Chapter, I will argue that the insights from that literature can be relevant also for tort law.

Building on recent findings in psychology and neuroscience, I analyze how IRBs can affect the creation, perception, and evaluation of different types of evidence in tort trials. In doing so, I draw a parallel between this literature and the neoclassical approach to discrimination. In addition, I discuss whether and to what extent implicit biases are likely to decrease accuracy in adjudication, i.e. whether they decrease the correspondence of courts' decisions to the facts underlying the dispute at trial (e.g., whether a certain harm was actually suffered by the victim). In this connection, I show that IRBs in the courtroom may hinder the achievement of deterrence even when they increase accuracy. This analysis aims to inform scholars and policy makers in, respectively, the study and the choice between tort law, regulation, and Pigovian taxes for addressing issues of distributive justice and efficiency in a wide spectrum of settings, ranging from environmental liability to product liability. Lastly, I discuss various policy responses to implicit biases in tort trials.

While reading this Chapter, it is important to keep in mind that research on IRBs and its usefulness for policy is debated in psychology. In this Chapter, I do

293 Graham Sandra and Brian Lowery, 2004. Priming Unconcious Racial Stereotypes About Adolescent Offenders, 28 LAW HUM. BEHAV 483; Jolls Christine and Cass Sunstein, 2006. The Law of Implicit Bias, 94 CAL. L. REV; Samuel Bagenstos, 2007. Implicit Bias, "Science" and Anti-Discrimination Law, 1 HARV. LAW REV, 1; Justin Levinson, 2007. Forgotten Racial Equality: Implicit Bias, Decisionmaking, and Misremembering, 57 DUKE L.J.; David Faigman, et al., 2008. A Matter of Fit: The Law of Discrimination and the Science of Implicit Bias, 59 Hastings L.J. 1389; Jeffrey Rachlinski et al., 2009. Does Unconscious Racial Bias Affect Trial Judges?, 84 NOTRE DAME L. REV. 1195; Justin Levinson et al., 2010. Guilty By Implicit Racial Bias: The Guilty/Not Guilty Implicit Association Test, 8 OHIO STATE J. CRIM. LAW, 187; Justin Levinson and Danielle Young, 2010. Different Shades of Bias: Skin Tone, Implicit Racial Bias, and Judgments of Ambiguous Evidence, 307 W. VA. L. REV. 112; Graser Alexander and Ana Alfinito Vieira, 2015. Taming the Biased Black Box? On the Potential Role of Behavioral Realism in Anti-Discrimination Policy, 35(1) OXF. J. LEG. STUD 121. The judicial branches of California, Minnesota and North Dakota have launced programs to train judges on IRBs and on techniques aimed at counteracting their influence on courts' decision-making. See: http://www.ncsc.-org/ibeducation. According to The Wall Street Journal in 2014 one fifth of large employers with diversity programs in the US provided employees with a training on implicit biases, see on this: Joann Lublin, 2014 Bringing Hidden Biases Into the Light: Big Businesses Teach Staffers How 'Unconscious Bias' Impacts Decisions, The Wall Street Journal.

not delve into this debate, as others have done so in other outlets.[294] The reader should however be aware of the existence of various critiques to the research on IRBs, which should be accounted for in considering the aptness of the analysis proposed below to inform policy.

The Chapter is structured as follows: Section 2 introduces the economics of discrimination. Building on Section 2, Section 3 introduces the scientific work on IRBs and draws a parallel with the economics of discrimination. Section 4 illustrates how IRBs may affect the creation and evaluation of evidence in tort law trials. The effects of IRBs on the functioning of tort law systems, with a particular focus on accuracy and welfare maximization, are discussed in Section 5. Section 6 discusses potential policy responses to IRBs. Section 7 concludes.

4.2 The Economics of Discrimination: An Introduction

Neoclassical law and economics literature describes individuals involved in trials (for instance, judges, prosecutors, and lawyers) as rational agents.[295] A clear example of this approach is the efficient prosecutor model, according to which prosecutors maximize either deterrence or convictions.[296] With the growth of the field, the analysis has been refined to account for more nuanced dynamics of human decision-making. As I will show in the following, the legal scholarship on IRBs in trial settings can be seen as an extension of this endeavor.

---

294 Brownstein Michael et al., 2019. What Do Implicit Measures Measure? WILEY INTERDISCIPLINARY REVIEWS: COGNITIVE SCIENCE 1501; John Jost, 2019. The IAT Is Dead, Long Live The IAT: Context-Sensitive Measures of Implicit Attitudes Are Indispensable to Social and Political Psychology. 28(1) CURRENT DIRECTIONS IN PSYCHOLOGICAL SCIENCE 10; John Jost et al., 2009. The Existence of Implicit Bias is Beyond Reasonable Doubt: A Refutation of Ideological and Methodological Objections and Executive Summary of Ten Studies that No Manager Should Ignore, 29 RESEARCH IN ORGANIZATIONAL BEHAVIOR 39; Mitchell Gregory and Philip Tetlock, 2017. Popularity as a Poor Proxy for Utility. In PSYCHOLOGICAL SCIENCE UNDER SCRUTINY: RECENT CHALLENGES AND PROPOSED SOLUTIONS 164; Oswald Frederick et al., 2015. Using The IAT to Predict Ethnic and Racial Discrimination: Small Effect Sizes of Unknown Societal Significance, 108 (4) J. PERS. SOC. PSYCHOL 562.

295 McAdams Richard and Thomas Ulen, 2009. Criminal Behavioral Law and Economics. In: N. Garoupa (eds.) Criminal Law and Economics, EDWARD ELGAR, CHELTENHAM 403.

296 Nuno Garoupa, 2012. The Economics of Prosecutors. In: Harel A, K Hylton (eds). Research Handbook on the Economics of Criminal Law. EDWARD ELGAR, CHELTENHAM 231.

Important works in law and economics conceive group-based discrimination as the outcome of a rational mental process.[297] In this connection, law and economics traditionally distinguishes between two types of discrimination: taste based and statistical.[298] Taste based discrimination refers to discrimination based on a conscious attitude towards a certain social group and that is not related to the socially identified purpose of the judgment performed. Thus, for instance, in the context of a trial, a judge may decide to find a defendant negligent when she identifies him as an outgroup for a reason that has nothing to do with the purposes of tort law (e.g. efficiency or corrective justice), but instead with her distaste towards outgroup members. This distaste may sometimes be grounded on misinformation about the prevalence and/or the causes of the prevalence of a certain trait (e.g. recklessness) among individuals belonging to different racial groups. For instance, a judge may consciously associate black people as being on average more reckless than whites and (mistakenly) believe that these differences have a biological basis. On the ground of this belief a judge may consciously hold a more positive attitude towards whites than towards blacks. Here, by discriminating, the judge is maximizing her utility and therefore is behaving "rationally", even though this behavior does not increase social welfare.

Contrary to taste based discrimination, statistical discrimination is not based on negative attitudes. Like under taste based discrimination, also here the judge may consciously decide to be less lenient with a defendant belonging to a certain social group. Yet, statistical discrimination identifies this conduct when the agent behaves this way in order to achieve an aim other than express a negative attitude. For instance, imagine that at a certain point in history in a certain town, black people are indeed on average more reckless when driving than white people. Here the judge may decide to be less lenient with black defendants than with white defendants with the aim of improving the accuracy of her decisions (as explained above, accuracy is generally accepted as a key aim of adjudication). This behavior could be considered "rational" in the sense that the judge maximizes her utility (assuming that she wants to be accurate) by acting this way.

297 Richard Posner, 1989. An Economic Analysis of Sex Discrimination Laws. 56(4) UNIV. CHIC. LAW REV 1317.

298 Ibid.

This section has introduced discrimination as discussed in prominent works in the law and economics literature. The next section discusses the main psychological findings on IRBs and draws a parallel with the economics of discrimination.

4.3 IRBs: An Introduction

Contrary to consciously held racially-related beliefs studied in the economics literature mentioned above, IRBs are biases driven by automatic attitudes and stereotypes.[299] The term bias indicates a shift in the way in which individuals respond to a particular stimulus within a continuum of possible responses.[300] In this connection, a bias is implicit when it is automatic and/or unconscious.[301] While automatic means that the shift requires little attention and that it is not easily controllable, unconscious indicates that it is not traceable through introspection.[302]

IRBs can refer both to attitudes and to stereotypes. The latter are associations between a group of individuals and a trait.[303] Thus, for instance a person may associate Eastern Asians with great math skills. Conversely an attitude is a mental association between a group of individuals and either a positive or a negative valence.[304] For instance, an individual may have a general negative attitude towards persons of color. Despite being related, it is important to mark the difference between attitudes and stereotypes. Both phenomena can be either positive or negative, and holding a negative stereotype towards a racial group does not prevent an individual from having an overall positive attitude towards this group and vice versa.[305] Thus, a person may associate persons of color with crime (a negative stereotype), but have a positive attitude towards them. Similarly, a person may

---

299 Kang et al. (2012). Since IRBs are not consciously held beliefs about race as those considered in the early economic analysis of law, their study extends and complements this previous literature.

300 Greenwald (2006).

301 Payne and Gawronski (2012); Jan De Houwer et al., 2009. Implicit Measures: A Normative Analysis and Review, 135(3) PSYCHOL. BULL 357.

302 Greenwald Anthony and Mahzarin Banaji, 1995. Implicit Social Cognition: Attitudes, Self-esteem, and Stereotypes, 102 PSYCHOL REV 8.

303 Greenwald (2006).

304 Kang et al. (2012). In psychology the term valence refers to the direction of the association, which can be either positive or negative.

305 Kang J. et al. (2012).

have a positive stereotype towards Eastern Asians by associating them with hard-working, but have an overall negative attitude towards them.

Implicit attitudes and stereotypes are identified with the use of indirect measurement procedures. These techniques are deemed able to identify attitudes and stereotypes that self-reported measures may fail to determine due to, for instance, social desirability concerns or unawareness.[306] In this connection, discrimination based on IRBs can be different from the one performed on the basis of consciously held beliefs and attitudes. This is because a subject may end up discriminating an individual even when he would prefer not doing so.[307] Because of this, the type of discrimination deriving from implicit biases is fundamentally different from the one debated by neoclassical law and economics.

The main indirect measurement procedures adopted in implicit social cognition are the Implicit Association Test (hereafter IAT), affective priming, and in functional magnetic resonance imaging (hereafter fMRI).

In affective priming subjects are exposed to two types of stimuli (a target and a prime) and they are asked to categorize the target as either positive or negative.[308] To perform the task, the only relevant stimulus is the target, therefore the prime should not affect the behavior of the subjects. For instance, in studies on implicit racial attitudes, subjects are first exposed to pictures of black faces and white faces (the prime).[309] This exposure occurs subliminally, meaning that pictures are shown for a very short time (e.g. 200 milliseconds), so that they are processed only unconsciously.[310] Subsequently, subjects are exposed to a series of words (the target) and are asked to categorize them (positive/negative). When priming with a racial stimulus facilitates the categorization of the words as negative the subject is said to hold a negative attitude towards the group.[311]

The IAT allows testing the relative strength of implicit attitudes and stereotypes via the measurement of response latencies in the categorization of stimuli

---

306 Hofmann Wilhelm et al., 2005. A Meta-Analysis on the Correlation between the Implicit Association Test and Explicit Self-Report Measure, 31(10) PERS. SOC. PSYCHOL. BULL 1370.

307 Christine Jolls, 2007. Behavioral law and economics (No. w12879). NATIONAL BUREAU OF ECONOMIC RESEARCH 10.

308 Fazio Russell et al., 1995. Variability in Automatic Activation as an Unobtrusive Measure of Racial Attitudes: A Bona Fide Pipeline?, 69(6) J. PERS. SOC. PSYCHOL 1013.

309 Ibid.

310 Ibid.

311 Ibid.

into classes.[312] In particular, in a racial IAT part of the stimuli relates to racial groups (e.g. a name more commonly associated with a black/white person), while the remaining stimuli relate to other concepts (e.g. good/bad).[313] Subjects are repeatedly asked to categorize each stimulus (e.g. black name) as belonging to one of two dyads.[314] Thus, for instance, subjects are first asked to categorize good/bad concepts and black/white names as belonging to either the black/good or the white/bad dyad.[315] And, subsequently, the task is repeated with black/bad and white/good dyads. Differences in response time between different combinations of dyads indicate that a certain racial group is more easily associated with a certain concept. Another technique often employed in the implicit racial attitude domain is blood oxygen level-dependent contrast imaging in functional magnetic resonance imaging.[316] This physiological measure identities variations in oxygen levels in the blood present in different parts of the brain, which are positively correlated with activations of these areas. Thus, for instance, exposure to black faces has been shown to generate a greater activation of the amygdala in white patients (the amygdala is a part of the brain related to the processing of emotions). Therefore, this strand of research indicates that the exposure to different racial groups can trigger distinctive emotional states.[317]

IRBs are pervasive both in the general population and among judges. The large amount of data gathered through the online platform Project Implicit (http://implicit.harvard.edu), indicates that, in the period 2000-2006, 68% of the over 1 million participants in the race IAT showed stronger associations between people of color and bad than between whites and bad. Only 14%, part of the black participants in the sample,[318] showed the reverse pattern.[319] Interestingly, black

---

312 Greenwald Anthony et al., 1998. Measuring Individual Dieffrences in Implicit Cognition: The Implicit Association Test. 74(6) J. PERS. SOC. PSYCHOL 1464.

313 Ibid.

314 Ibid.

315 Ibid.

316 Fazio Russell and Michael Olson, 2003. Implicit Measures in Social Cognition Research: Their Meaning and Use. 54(1) ANNU. REV. PSYCHOL. 297.

317 Kubota Jennifer et al., 2012. The Neuroscience of Race. 15(7) NAT NEUROSCI 940.

318 Nosek Brian et al., 2007. Pervasiveness and Correlates of Implicit Attitudes and Stereotypes, 18 EUR. REV. SOC. PSYCHOL 36. This finding is consistent with previous literature showing that in the racial domain people tend to show a preference for their own ingroups, see on this: Miles Hewstone et al., 2002. Integroup Bias, 53 ANNU. REV. PSYCHOL. 575.

319 Nosek et al. (2007).

participants were the only group that did not show a strong pro-white preference.[320] While most participants to these studies were US citizens, also Europeans (both from continental Europe and the UK), took part in the IAT. The analysis of those data shows the absence of significant differences in responses provided by Europeans and US citizens.[321] It is important to stress that these results come from a self-selected sample of visitors of the Implicit Project website and therefore they can-not be considered a sample representative of the distribution of attitudes of a particular population. However, the large size and the diversity of the sample likely makes it more representative of most samples used in laboratory experiments. This may hold also with regards to the European population for which the availability of the website exclusively in English decreases the representativeness of the population.[322] These considerations provide support that studies based on IAT are relevant also to understand the judgment and decision-making of Europeans.

With regards to judges, despite the fact that society expects them to be free from these biases, there is no evidence that suggests that they are immune or even differently affected by IRBs than the general population.[323] In a three stages experiment consisting in a racial IAT, and two vignettes studies - one in which racial information was subliminally primed and the other in which it was made explicit- Rachlinski and co-authors found that a large majority (87.1%) of white participants showed an implicit attitude more favorable towards whites than towards people of color.[324] These findings are consistent with results obtained with non-judges. This was confirmed by the finding that also black judges did not show a clear preference for whites or people of color. 44.2% of them showed a preference for white individuals, but, in general, preferences were not particularly strong.[325]

Similar patterns are observed in studies on medical doctors, confirming that large proportions of white individuals show implicit attitudes favorable to white

---

320 Ibid.

321 Ibid..

322 See on this: Nosek et al. (2007).

323 For a strong case on the effect of IRBs on courts' decisions, see also: Papillon Kimberly, 2013. The Court's Brain: Neuroscience and Judicial Decision Making in Criminal Sentencing, 49 COURT REVIEW 48.

324 Rachlinski et al. (2009).

325 Rachlinski et al. (2009).

people.[326] Also these studies show that black people tend, on average, to be race neutral.[327] These studies are of particular relevance here because, like judges, medical doctors are highly educated individuals that are expected to operate in a racially neutral manner. These data and the similarities between the two professions support the claim that judges are not differently affected by IRBs than the general population.

The implicitness, especially the uncontrollability and the unconsciousness characteristic, of these biases implies that, sometimes, individuals that would find it inappropriate to hold these implicit racial attitudes and stereotypes, might nonetheless involuntarily act upon them. Thus a person may think that she likes people of color and that it is appropriate to hold this attitude, but her implicit attitude might go in the other direction, perhaps leading her to act negatively towards them.[328]

4.4 IRBs and Evidence in Tort Trials

The occurrence of an accident can give rise to a legal dispute. When this happens, parties have the right to present evidence to the court and the court is expected to use this evidence to determine the truthfulness of the statements made by parties regarding facts that are relevant for the case.[329] Evidence law regulates when, how, and what evidence can be presented by whom and how courts are required to process this information.

---

326 For a study with a sample of more than 2500 US medical doctors see: Sabin Janice et al., 2009. Physicians' Implicit and Explicit Attitudes About Race by MD Race, Ethnicity, and Gender, 20(3) J. HEALTH CARE POOR UNDERSERVED 896. See also: Green Alexander et al. 2007. Implicit Bias Among Physicians and Its Prediction of Thrombolysis Decisions for Black and White Patients, 22(9) J. GEN. INTERN. MED 1231; Sabin Janice et al., 2008. Physician Implicit Attitudes and Stereotypes About Race and Quality of Medical Care, 46(7) MEDICAL CARE 678; Blair Irene et al., 2008. An Investigation of Associations Between Clinicians' Ethnic or Racial Bias and Hypertention Treatment, Medication Adherence and Blood Pressure Control, 29(7) J. GEN. INTERN. MED 990.

327 Sabin et al. (2009). See also: Green et al. (2007); Sabin (2008).

328 Kang et al. (2012). Please notice, that the effect of IRBs on behavior is still contested in the literature, see Brownstein et al. (2019); Mitchell and Tetlock (2017).

329 Taruffo (2014).

Evidence at trial may regard both brute facts and facts evaluatively determined. Brute facts are those that have only an empirical dimension,[330] such as the collision of two vehicles. With regards to brute facts, the evidence provides information to the court regarding whether and how the fact occurred. Conversely, facts evaluatively determined have an evaluative dimension that is established by legal norms.[331] Thus, for instance, a particular conduct (which has an empirical dimension) can be considered reasonable or not (the evaluative dimension). In this case the evidence is concerned with whether and how the fact occurred and subsequently the fact is evaluated according to the relevant legal norm.

The contention of this section is that studies in implicit social cognition suggest that IRBs can affect courts' perception of both brute and evaluative determined facts.

4.4.1 The Presentation and Evaluation of Brute Facts

Procedural rules distinguish between the moment in which parties present the evidence to the court and the time in which the latter is required to evaluate which of the facts have been proved. In this section, I shall follow this distinction for the purpose of the analysis.[332] The contention of this section is that the influence of IRBs on courts' assessment of the evidence can already begin in the phase of the trail in which evidence is presented.

4.4.1.1 Implicit Biases and the Presentation of Evidence

A common distinction is usually drawn between two types of evidence depending on whether the item of evidence is created within or outside the trial. The latter is usually referred to as pre-constituted evidence and refers mainly to documents that are formed before the trial begins, such as a medical report on the injuries suffered by the victim of an accident. The former refers instead to items of evidence that

330 Ibid.

331 Ibid.

332 From a psychological perspective, some of the tasks performed by adjudicators during the phase of the presentation of evidence are already evaluative in nature. This is clear, for instance, with regards to the evaluation of the credibility of a witness testimony. Yet, since in this Chapter I review and categorize the psychological literature on IRBs that is relevant for the study of evidence law, in the following, I will refer to the two phases of the trial by using labels borrowed by procedural law.

do not exist before the trial begins and that are instead formed at the trial. Evidence that is created at the trial can take various forms such as witness testimony, party interrogations, decisory oaths, deeds, confessions, etc. I will argue in the following that courts' perception of both evidence created at trial and pre-constituted evidence can be affected by IRBs.

4.4.1.1.1 Brute Facts, IRBs and the Creation of Evidence at the Trial

A central feature of the evidence that is created at trial is that courts are required to evaluate whether the items of evidence so generated can be used as a reliable source for establishing whether a particular fact occurred. With regards to some type of evidence (e.g. testimony and parties' interrogation) an obvious criterion that informs this evaluation is whether the person that reported the information is credible. [333]

Building on case law analysis, legal scholars have long argued that IRBs often lead white judges (or juries, e.g. in the US) to trust a testimony given by a black individual less than one provided by a white witness.[334] This conclusion is supported by recent experimental findings. Stanley and co-authors have tested whether a racial Implicit Association Test (IAT) predicts explicit evaluations of the trustworthiness of faces.[335] They find that individuals that showed a strong implicit bias in favor of whites tended to consider black faces less trustworthy than white faces.[336] These findings suggest that in the context of a trial, the evidence provided by a black party to a white judge could be, ceteris paribus, less likely to be found credible than the evidence provided by a white party. This literature suggests that IRBs may bias judges' perception of evidence presented at trial, potentially reducing the ability of minorities to present evidence in their favor, for instance, during an interrogation.

---

333 This power is conferred to the judge under, for instance, Italian and French law. See on this: Jean Vincent and Serge Guinchard, 2003. Procédure Civile DALLOZ 768; Michele Taruffo, 2012. La Prova nel Processo Civile, GIUFFRÈ EDITORE 424.

334 See on this: Carpenter Elliot, 2002. The Hearsay Rule and Racial Evaluations of Credibility 8(1) WASHINGTON AND LEE JOURNAL OF CIVIL RIGHTS AND SOCIAL JUSTICE 15.

335 Stanley Damian et al., 2011. Implicit Race Attitudes Predict Trustworthiness Judgment and Economic Trust Decisions, 108(19) PNAS 7710.

336 Ibid.

Legal systems differ in terms of the evidentiary function of the interrogation.[337] For instance, under Italian law, the *interrogatorio libero* can only provide judges with *argomenti di prova*, which is an item of evidence that has the lowest degree of probative value.[338] A similar regime regulates the *comparution personnelle* in France.[339] However, other forms of parties' interrogation provide items of evidence with a higher degree of probative value, such as the Italian *interrogatorio formale* and the *Parteivernehmung* in Germany.[340] Depending on the regime regulating parties' interrogations and on the extent to which judges follow these rules when deciding cases, the influence of IRBs on courts' perception of evidence provided during an interrogation may have a variable importance in determining the outcome of the case.

4.4.1.1.2 Brute Facts, IRBs and Pre-Constituted Evidence

The second way in which parties can provide evidence to support their claims is to present evidence that was created outside the trial. My contention here is that IRBs can affect the creation of this evidence and the item of evidence so generated is likely to bring the effects of the bias to the decision of the court. In this connection, an example that is particularly meaningful in the realm of tort law concerns courts' evaluation of the losses that need to be compensated to the victim.

One of the constituents of a tort is that the victim has suffered a loss. The harm can take various forms, and the law often traces a general distinction between economic and non-economic losses. While the former refers to losses of money or other goods purchased in markets (income, properties, medical services, etc.), the latter identifies losses in utility deriving from the destruction of irreplaceable things, such as pain, emotional distress, loss of amenity, etc.[341]

Whether, and to what extent, a victim of a tort has suffered a loss is one of the facts that needs to be proved at trial. Medical reports often play a major role in

337 For an analysis of parties' interrogation in Europe from a comparative perspective see: Taruffo (2014).

338 On the Parteivernehmung and the interrogatorio formale see Taruffo (2014).

339 Taruffo (2014). On the regime of compaurition personnelle in France see Christophe Lefort, 2012. Procédure Civile, DALLOZ, 347.

340 Taruffo (2014).

341 For a review of non-economic losses in the EU in a comparative perspective see generally: Horton Rogers (eds), 2001. Damages for Non-Pecuniary Loss in a Comparative Perspective, SPRINGER; Giovanni Comandé, 2006. Towards a Global Model for Adjudicating Personal Injury Damages: Bridging Europe and the United States, 19(2) TEMPLE INT. COMP. LAW J. 241.

providing courts with information on these facts both regarding the amount of medical expenses that a victim had to bear because of the accident, and the non-economic losses that a victim is likely to have suffered.[342] This makes the study of the influence of implicit biases on the creation of medical reports relevant for the study of tort law.

Evidence indicates that in both the EU and the US health care system members of ethnic minorities often receive inadequate or inferior medical treatment compared to the one provided to white patients.[343] Experimental evidence suggests that IRBs might be one of the causes of these discriminative treatments.[344] The relevance of IRBs to determine patients' treatment is, however, debated in the literature. Some studies found strong evidence of the impact of IRBs on patient treatments,[345] while others found mixed[346] or no correlation between the two measures.[347]

---

342 Comandé (2006). On the practice of using medical scores to help judges assessing damages for pain at trial see: THE LAW COMMISSION REPORT NO 257 Damages for Non-Pecuniary Loss (1999) para 3.190-3.194.

343 Regarding the EU see: Bhopal Raj, 2007. Racism in Health and Health Care in Europe: Reality or Mirage? 17(3) EUR. J. PUBLIC HEALTH 238; FRA, 2013. Inequalities and Multiple Discrimination in Access to and Quality of Healthcare. With regards to the situation in the US see: Shavers Vickie et al., 2012. Research on Race/Ethnicity and Health Care Discrimination: Where We Are and Where We Need to Go, 102(5) AM. J. PUBLIC HEALTH 930. With regards to pain treatment see: Mathur Vani et al., 2014. Racial Bias in Pain Perception and Response: Experimental Examination of Automatic and Deliberate Processes, 15(5) J. PAIN 476; Cintron Alexie and Sean Morrison, 2006. Pain and Ethnicity in the United States: A Systematic Review, 9 J. PALLIAT. MED 1454; Burgess Diana et al., 2014. The Effect of Cognitive Load and Patient Race on Physician's Decisions to Prescribe Opiods for Chronic Low Back Pain: A Randomized Trial, 15 PAIN MEDICINE 965.

344 Sabin Janice and Anthony Greenwald, 2012. The Influence of Implicit Bias on Treatment Recommendations for 4 Common Pediatric Conditions: Pain, Urinary Tract Infection, Attention Deficit Hyperactivity Disorder, and Asthma, 102(5) AM. J. PUBLIC HEALTH 988; Sabin et al. (2008); Burgess et al. (2007).

345 Sabin and Greenwald (2012) .

346 Sabin et al. (2008); Burgess et al (2014).

347 Haider Adil et al., 2011. Association of Unconscious Race and Social Class Bias with Vignette-based Clinical Assessments by Medical Students, 306 JAMA 942; Hirsh Adam et al., 2015. The Interaction of Patient Race, Provider Bias, and Clinical Ambiguity on Pain Management Decisions 16(6) JOP 558.

Within the domain of pain medicine and treatment, a study with 86 academic pediatricians it was found that IRBs affect pain treatments.[348] The higher the implicit pro-white racial biases held by pediatricians, the lower was the prescription of pain narcotic to black patients. Conversely, the magnitude of the bias was not related to differences in pain treatment of white individuals.[349]

Findings of racially dependent differences in pain perception of in-group/out-group individuals have been confirmed by neuroscientific studies. These studies have shown greater activations of empathy related areas of the brain when the observer is exposed to images/videos showing members of his racial group suffering pain than when the person in pain is a member of a different racial group.[350] In one of these studies it was shown that IRBs predicted the activation of the left anterior insula, which is considered to be a part of the brain that is involved in the perception of third parties' pain.[351]

Overall the existing empirical literature suggests that IRBs might play a role in determining discriminative medical treatments in the health care system.

Furthermore, these studies testify that, in the context of a trial, the evidence that is brought to court, sometimes labeled in the literature as 'objective',[352] might not be immune to the influence of IRBs. This evidence may also influence the award of damages by courts. For instance, the assessment of the pain suffered by a victim as 'moderate' as opposed to 'severe' may affect the pain and suffering damages the court awards.[353]

Medical reports are just an example of evidence created outside the trial that is not immune from IRBs. Evidence suggests that US police officers are as affected as other individuals by IRBs.[354] Some of this research suggests that IRBs are able

---

348 Sabin and Greenwald (2012).

349 Ibid.

350 Xu Xiaojing et al., 2009. Do You Feel My Pain? Racial Group Membership Modulates Empathic Neural Responses, 29 NEUROSCIENCE 8525; Azevedo et al. (2012).

351 Azevedo et al. (2012).

352 Comandé (2006). For a suggestion of using medical reports to establish pain and suffering awards as a remedy to the biases that affects judges and juries, see: Avraham, 2006. Putting a Price on Pain-and-Suffering Damages: A Critique of the Current Approaches and a Preliminary Proposal for Change, 100(1) NORTHWEST. UNIV. LAW REV 87.

353 Notice also that differences in medical perception of pain caused by IRBs may also affect the creation of evidence at the trial when medical experts are called to assess the medical conditions of a victim of an accident during the trial.

354 For a review of this literature see: Kang (2012).

to shift policemen's visual attention. For instance, it has been shown that priming policemen with a black male face increases the speed with which they recognize the figure of a weapon that emerges out of a static image on a video.[355] These results, coupled with the literature on IRBs and trust,[356] suggest that police reports might be affected by IRBs. These reports, when presented as evidence at trial, are likely to impact courts' decisions. An example of this is the report of a police officer regarding the dynamics of a car accident that is used at trial to support the claim that the accident occurred in a certain manner. This, in turn, can affect the determination of causation and negligence in a tort law trial.

4.4.1.2 Implicit Biases and the Evaluation of Evidence Regarding Brute Facts

After the phase relative to the presentation of evidence, procedural law requires judges to evaluate the epistemic status of the statements made by parties in light of the evidence that has been presented. In contemporary Civil Law and Common Law systems the principle of free evaluation of evidence is the core rule for the evaluation of evidence.[357] According to this principle the evaluation of the evidence should be made by the judge on a case by case basis and according to his discretion.[358] Some study suggest that this activity might be influenced by IRBs.

In establishing the truthfulness of a statement at trial, courts are often required to consider multiple and contrasting pieces of evidence. This may leave uncertainty regarding whether, given the evidence presented, the fact can be considered proven. Empirical studies suggest that the evaluation of ambiguous evidence might be affected by IRBs.[359] In a study by Levinson and Young it has been shown that in a robbery case, when evidence is ambiguous, showing a photo of an alleged offender with darker skin (compared to the one shown in the control group), increases the degree by which the evidence is evaluated as proving guilt.[360] Racial IAT scores predicted evidence judgment.[361] Conversely, explicit racial preferences

---

355 Eberhardt Jennifer et al., 2004. Seeing Black: Race, Crime, and Visual Processing, 87 J. PERS. SOC. PSYCHOL 876.

356 See supra.

357 See: Taruffo (2014).

358 Ibid.

359 Levinson and Young (2010).

360 Ibid.

361 Ibid.

(i.e. preferences consciously held) were not found to correlate with it.[362] These results were corroborated in another study, which showed that implicit associations between person of color and guilt predicted judgments on the probative value of ambiguous evidence in a mock criminal case.[363]

4.4.2 The Evaluation of Facts Evaluatively Determined

The evaluation of the evidence concerning brute facts does not exhaust the type of evaluative tasks that a judge is called to undertake in order to reach a decision. Another form of evaluation that a judge has to make is concerned with so called facts evaluatively determined, meaning facts that are defined by legal norms that contain an evaluative term. In the following, I will argue that also this type of evaluation might be affected by IRBs.

In a tort law context, under a negligence rule, a fact evaluatively determined that plays a major role in determining the outcome of a dispute is whether the alleged tortfeasor took due care by acting as a reasonable person. However, what a reasonable person would have done in that situation, often remains vague in legal practice. A growing strand of literature shows that when legal standards are vague, they can be unconsciously shifted to protect in-group members.[364] Standard shifting is a result of motivated cognition, meaning the unconscious tendency to acquire, understand and elaborate information in a way that is consistent with the preferences of the observer.[365] Experimental evidence shows that these preferences may derive from the desire to protect racially identified in-group members.[366] This occurs as an unconscious reaction to the threat that an accusation of immoral/illegal conduct of one of the members of a group brings to the social status of the group as a whole.[367] IRBs seem to have a role in determining standard

---

362 Ibid.

363 Levinson et al. (2007).

364 Miron Anca et al., 2010. Motivated Shifting of Justice Standards, 20(10) PERS. SOC. PSYCHOL. BULL 1; Leidner Bernhard and Emanuele Castano, 2012. Morality Shifting in the Context of Intergroup Violence, 42(1) EUR. J. SOC. PSYCHOL 82; Tarrant Mark et al., 2012. Social Identity and Perceptions of Torture: It's Moral When We Do It, 48(2) J. EXP. SOC. PSYCHOL 513.

365 Kunda Ziva, 1990. The Case for Motivated Reasoning, 108(3) PSYCHOL BULL 480.

366 Miron (2010).

367 Ibid.

shifting.[368] In particular, Shoda and co-authors show that the greater the degree of dissonance between implicit and explicit biases held towards people of color, the greater the standard shifting.[369] In other words, people whose explicit racial attitudes are relatively more positive and whose implicit racial attitudes are relatively more negative, are more likely to engage in stronger standard shifting. This would be due to the fact that greater degrees of difference between the two measures lead to more effortful processing of information, which in turn leads to more motivated reasoning.[370]

Legal scholarship on motivated cognition has grown rapidly in recent years,[371] gaining recognition also in the literature on law and IRBs.[372] The study by Shoda offers the missing link between the two strands of literature, showing how IRBs relate to standard shifting. This is a first study, and further evidence on the relationship between the two phenomena needs to be gathered before strong claims can be made.

In a tort law context, besides altering the amount of evidence needed to consider a brute fact as proved,[373] standard shifting can occur in the establishment of the due care standard. In practice, this shift may materialize in courts' asking more evidence to prove that a conduct was reasonable when the alleged tortfeasor is an in-group member and the defendant is an out-group member than when both parties are in-group or out-group members.

---

368 Shoda Tonya, 2014. Having Explicit-Implicit Evaluation Discrepancies Triggers Race-Based Motivated Reasoning, 32(2) SOC. COGN 190.

369 Ibid.

370 Ibid. See also: Shoda Tonya et al., 2014. Implicit Consistency Processes in Social Cognition: Explicit-Implicit Discrepancies Across Systems of Evaluation, 8(3) SOC. PSYCHOL. PERS. SCI 135.

371 For a review of this literature see: Sood Avani, 2013. Motivated Cognition in Legal Judgments – An Analytic Review, 9 ANN REV. L. SOC. SCI. 307.

372 Kang and colleagues argue that motivated reasoning may affect the way in which white judges evaluate brute facts when one of the parties at trial is black and the other party and the judge are white. In particular, they claim that standard shifting can lead the white judge to require more evidence from the side of the black party to prove items of evidence that support her statements, see: Kang (2012).

373 Ibid.

4.5 The Effect of IRBs on the Functioning of Tort Law

In the previous section it has been argued that IRBs may affect the type of evidence presented at trial, the way in in which judges perceive and evaluate it, and how decisions are consequently made in tort law contexts. Building on this analysis this section discusses how implicit biases may decrease the actual and perceived probability for a member of a discriminated group to obtain full compensation at trial. In addition, it analyzes how the existence of IRBs in trial settings can hinder the achievement of optimal deterrence. In particular, the analysis focuses on the distorting effects that IRBs may have on the incentives that tort law provides to reduce negative externalities and the link between accuracy, deterrence, and IRBs.

4.5.1 Setting the Stage

The analysis of the effect of IRBs on the deterrent capacity of tort law has, as a natural antecedent, the description of a society in which tort law regulates the behavior of its members.

In the following, for reasons of simplicity, to better capture the effect of IRBS on trial systems, I will make some assumptions regarding the society in which my analysis takes place. In particular, I will assume that this society has the following characteristics: first, there are only two racial groups. I will refer to one of the two groups as to non-discriminated group and to the other one as to discriminated group. Second, all judges in the society are members of one of the two groups. In the following, I will assume that judges are all members of the non-discriminated group. Third, a proportion of victims and tortfeasors are members of the non-discriminated group and the remaining part are members of the discriminated group. Fourth, members of the two groups establish the affiliation of an individual to one of the two groups by looking at some trait of the physical appearance of the observed individual (such as skin color, facial traits, etc.) or other potentially relevant characteristics such as the name of the person.

To the extent that the society described above represents a good approximation of the relevant aspects of a society in a given country, the conclusions reached below can describe the effects of IRBs on the functioning of tort law in that society.

Looking at the composition of judiciaries in Europe, existing studies suggest that the presence of non-white judges within the EU is very limited. Given that exact data on the number of non-white judges are not available in most Civil Law countries, we need to find proxies for this measure. Ethnicity is arguably a good proxy for this. In this regard, a recent study by de Rechtspraak has concluded that in Germany, France and the Netherlands very few judges have a migrant background.[374] For instance, in Germany, where people with Turkish origins are the largest ethnic minority, there are only five judges with Turkish names out of the 21.000 judges operating in the country.[375] In addition, the analysis of the trends of law students/lawyers operating in the three countries confirm that members of minority groups are not numerous in the respective judiciary and suggests that, at least in the near future, these numbers are not likely to increase.[376] These studies highlight that the assumptions made in here can a fair approximation of the reality prevailing in many contemporary societies throughout Europe.

4.5.2 The Effects of IRBs on Deterrence

In the following, I will discuss two main effects of IRBs in the courtroom, meaning, direct harm and signaling direct harm. This analysis is useful to study of the effects of IRBs on the functioning of tort law systems.

4.5.2.1 Direct Harm and Implicit Biases

Direct harm is here defined as a loss that stems directly from the judgment of a judge. In the context of the present analysis, direct harm can be defined as the difference between the situation that the member of the discriminated group experiences if the judgment of a judge is affected by IRBs, and the situation in

374 Anita Böcker and Leny de Groot-van Leeuwen, 2007. Ethnic Minorities Representation in the Judiciary: Diversity among Judges in Old and New Countries of Immigration, THE JUDICIARY QUARTERLY, 22.

375 Note that in Germany there are more than 2.5 million persons with Turkish origins and that in the country there are 25,5 judges per 100000 heads of population. However, my point here is not that individuals with Turkish origins are underrepresented in the judiciary (which is, however, arguably true). My point here is, instead, that they are very few.

376 The analysis of trends in numbers of individual members of ethnic minorities studying law or working as lawyers is relevant for understanding the likely composition of judiciaries in the near future because legal education and having worked as a qualified lawyer for a certain number of years are prerequisite to become judges in many EU countries. Böcker and de Groot-van Leeuwen (2007).

which the same person would have been, had the judgment of the judge not been influenced by the bias.

Based on the types of effect that they have, it is useful to distinguish two different types of direct harm caused by IRBs.

First, direct harm can be measured as the difference in the likelihood that a member of a discriminated group obtains unbiased compensation at trial given the presence or the absence of IRBs in the judiciary (hereafter: probability harm).[377] In Section 4 I have highlighted that, in the context of civil trials, IRBs may affect the way in which judges evaluate the epistemic status of the statements made by parties regarding brute facts and facts evaluatively determined. Thus, probability harm is a decrease in the probability that a statement made by a party will be considered as proved. In the context of tort law, this harm can materialize in a discriminated person losing a case that she would have not otherwise lost or receiving a lower compensation than in absence of the bias.

Second, probability harm can give rise to a suffering of the member of the discriminated group when this individual perceives its effects and starts believing that he has been discriminated against (hereafter: discrimination harm). This suffering can be conceived as a cost that members of discriminated groups bear when they bring a case to trial.

4.5.2.2 Implicit Bias and Signalling Direct Harm

Signalling direct harm is defined here as harm (deriving from the fact that courts are racially biased) that can be perceived by potential parties at trial.

As noted in the previous section, discrimination that causes probability harm can be a product of a decision made by judges when evaluating evidence. Members of discriminated groups may or may not be aware of being harmed in such way. They may observe that winning a case is (more) difficult (than in absence of the bias), but they may not realize that part of this difficulty is due to a bias that influences how judges make decisions. This is because how the judge reaches a decision on the evaluation of the evidence is not observable by third parties. In fact, this is often a mental process of the judge and in situations in which decisions are

377 Biased compensation is every level of compensation that is lower than what would have been awarded in absence of the bias. Biased compensation is zero when IRBs lead the member of the discriminated group to lose a case. Alternatively, biased compensation is a positive level of compensation that is however lower than the one that would have been received otherwise.

collegial, this deliberation often occurs in the secret of the chamber.[378] The scarce, and not necessarily transparent, information offered by the motivation of the decision is often not informative in this regard.

The low observability of probability harm does not imply that members of discriminated group cannot believe that they have lost a case because they have been discriminated against. It is in fact clear that an individual can always find various explanations for the "why" he has lost at trial. These explanations can be grounded on other beliefs. For instance, a member of a discriminated group can always explain having lost at trial with the racism of the judge, even when they do not observe the decision-making process of the judge. In these cases, the party previous belief "judges are racist", might find greater confirmation in the increase in trials that members of discriminated groups lose because of the effect of IRBs.

4.5.3 Impact Size on Trial Outcomes

The size of the impact of implicit biases on trial outcomes is debated in the literature.[379] Most studies on the impact of IRBs on behavior have been carried out in laboratory settings where situational factors that may reduce the effect of IRBs on human behavior are not present.[380] On the other hand, even if the influence of IRBs on human behavior in a single situation in real life circumstances is limited, the overall effect is not necessarily trivial.[381] This is because single small effects can have a non-trivial impact when the same person is repeatedly subject to the effect of the bias (so called cumulative effect).[382]

In the trial settings the cumulative effect is determined by the number of occurrences in a trial in which IRBs may influence the creation, perception and evaluation of evidence, as compared to the situation in absence of the bias. Thus, for instance, the creation of a biased medical report by a physician that is subsequently used as evidence at trial is one occurrence of IRBs, the court's biased perception

378 This occurs, for instance, both under the Italian and the Dutch system of civil procedure.

379 Mitchell and Tetlock (2007).

380 Ibid.

381 Greenwald Anthony et al., 2015. Statistically Small Effects of the Implicit Association Test Can HaveSocietally Large Effects 108(4) J. PERS. SOC. PSYCHOL 553; Jerry Kang, 2014. Rethinking Intent and Impact: Some Behavioral Realism About Equal Protection, 66(3) ALA L REV 627.

382 Greenwald et al. (2015); Kang (2014).

of the report during the presentation of evidence is a second, et cetera. The cumulative effect in a trial in which the judge and one of the parties are members of the non-discriminated group and the other party is a member of the discriminated group is found by comparing the expected probability for an individual to fail to obtain full compensation given that she is either a member of a discriminated group or not.

Imagine a hypothetical scenario in which a victim sues a tortfeasor for damages. In order to win the case he will have to prove five facts.[383] When the victim bears the burden of proof, the failure to prove one or more of these facts results in losing the case. Imagine also that the victim brings to trial five items of evidence, each of which is meant to prove the truthfulness of one of the statements concerning each of the five relevant facts. In addition, the victim has a certain probability of proving that each fact occurred as he stated.[384] Because of the effect of IRBs on courts' perception and evaluation of evidence, this probability might be lower when the victim is a member of the discriminated group than if he is a member of the non-discriminated group. Since this probability is lower for each fact that has to be proved, and that the proof of each fact is a necessary condition to obtain compensation, even small decreases in the probability to prove each individual fact can substantially reduce the overall chances for a member of a discriminated group to win at trial.

Note also that, in a tort law trial, the proof of one fact can be relevant for the establishment of multiple constituents of a tort. Thus, for instance, as mentioned above, the police report regarding the dynamics of a car accident can be used at trial to prove both causation and negligence. In this case, when a particular conduct is regulated by negligence law the effect of the bias on the probability to obtain compensation can be even larger than when the report is used to prove a single necessarily element of the tort. This is because the decrease in probability to prove each fact will be repeated for multiple tort elements that need to be proved. In other words, even if the plaintiff was able to prove one element with the use of this information, there is still a possibility that the same information might not be sufficient to prove the other element.

---

383 For simplicity I will assume here that the activity of the tortfeasor is not able to affect the probability of the victim to win the case.

384 One can argue that claims can only be formulated in probabilistic terms anyway, see Alessandro Romano, 2016. God's Dice: The Law in a Probalistic World, 41(1) UNIV. DAYT. LAW REV 57.

4.5.4 IRBs and Deterrence

As discussed above, tort law is a legal tool that can be used to steer human behavior. By imposing liability, policymakers may try to influence the investments in precautionary measures and levels of activity of individuals that, through their conducts, impose negative externalities on third parties. In this perspective, tort law has, therefore, a deterrent function. This section analyzes whether and how, IRBs in the judiciary alter the deterrent capacity of tort law. Since from an economic perspective optimal deterrence is seen as a primary aim of tort law, this analysis is of relevance also for law and economics scholarship.

4.5.4.1 IRBs and Tort Law When the Victim is a Member of a Discriminated Group

In this section, I focus on the situation in which the victim is a member of the discriminated group. One of the distinguishing characteristics of tort law is that its functioning relies on victims' initiative to bring a case to trial and on their ability to win at trial.[385] A party's willingness to litigate a case depends on the expected value from litigation.[386] The greater the expected benefit and the lower the costs (measured in utility), the more an individual is willing to litigate a case.

In the previous section it has been argued that IRBs in the judiciary expose members of discriminated group to the risk of suffering direct harm in the form of a lower probability of winning a case and a higher probability of receiving a lower compensation. Implicit biases might also signal them the existence of this risk. Thus direct harm reduces both the actual and the perceived expected value of litigating a case. This implies that IRBs are likely to reduce both the number of cases that victims bring to court and victims' probability to win or receive unbiased compensation at trial.

Note, in addition, that the direct harm suffered by a victim is often not necessarily independent from the racial group of the alleged tortfeasor.[387] For instance,

---

385 De facto, victims often ask relief for the suffered harm directly to the tortfeasor before bringing the case to trial. This may end up in an attempt to settle the case outside courts. The case of settlements is not considered in the present work.

386 William Landes, 1971. An Economic Analysis of the Courts, 14 J. LAW ECON 61.

387 In line with this statement substantial evidence from the field shows that, in the criminal context, sentencing decisions are not independent from the race of the victim, with crimes perpetuated against white victims being punished more harshly than crimes in which the victim is a person

in the case of motivated reasoning, a judge may shift the standard of proof to protect in-group members. More in general, the expected benefit of litigating a case is also dependent on the ability of the adversary to effectively convince the judge of the truthfulness of the version of the facts that is more favorable to her. In this regard, the membership of the tortfeasor to the same racial group of the judge puts the member of the discriminated group in a situation of even greater disadvantage than if the tortfeasor belonged to the discriminated group.

The reduction in number of cases brought to trial and in the likelihood for a member of a discriminated group to receive unbiased compensation implies that, ceteris paribus, tortfeasors are more likely to escape liability in presence of an implicit bias than otherwise. In addition, tortfeasors who are member of the non-discriminated group are more likely to escape liability than tortfeasors of the discriminated group.

The economics of tort law tells us that, both under strict liability and negligence, the ability of the tortfeasor to escape liability reduces her incentives to take precautionary measures.[388] In the context of the present analysis, this implies that when the victim of an accident is a member of a discriminated group, tortfeasors may receive lower incentives to take precautionary measures and/or lead her to increase his activity level than in absence of the bias. Note that these effects might be greater when the tortfeasor is a member of the non-discriminated group than when both parties are members of the discriminated group. In both cases, if in absence of the bias tortfeasors had incentives to take optimal care and/or optimally engage in the activity level, IRBs decrease the efficiency of the system. To illustrate, consider the graph below.

of color. See on this: U.S. Gov't Accountability Office, GAO GGD-90-557, Death Penalty Sentencing: Research Indicates Pattern of Racial Disparities, 1990,5; Glaeser, Edward and Bruce Sacerdote, 2003. Sentencing in Homicide Cases and the Roles of Vengeance, 32 J. LEG. STUD 363.

388 Kahan Marcel, 1989. Causation and Incentives to Take Care Under Negligence Rule, 18 J. LEG STUD 427; Louis Kaplow and Stephen Shavell, (2002) Economic Analysis of Law, in Handbook of Public Economics (A.J Auerbach and M. Feldstein Eds.), Vol. 3, ELSEVIER SCIENCE B.V., p. 1669.

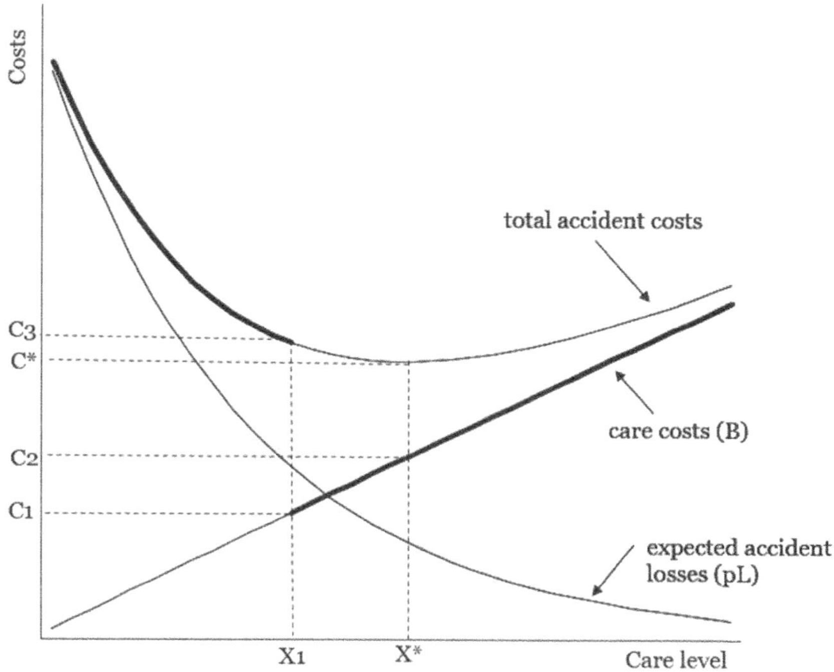

Figure 1 Social cost of accidents when victim is member of discriminated group.

Imagine an activity regulated via a negligence rule. In absence of IRBs, judges impose liability at level X* where the social cost of accidents is the lowest (C*). If the court due to IRBs sets a too low due care standard at X1, the injurer will follow this too low level, because then his care costs are only C1 instead of C2. However, at X1 total accident costs (C3) are higher than at X (C*)

Note, in addition, that the variation in the deterrent effectiveness of tort law may depend also on the distribution of the harm across the racial groups composing the population of victims.

A population of victims is here defined as the group of individuals that are legally entitled to ask damages to a tortfeasor for a given harm. In a society as the one described in Section 5.1, the population of victims can be differently composed in terms of percentages of members of the discriminated and the non-discriminated group. The greater is the proportion of the harm imposed on members of the discriminated group in the population of victims, the more IRBs in the judiciary can decrease the effectiveness of tort law to achieve deterrence. To illustrate, take the example of a company that discharges toxic waste in an area inhabited by both members of a discriminated group and members of the non-discriminated group. This activity imposes an expected harm of 100 to a population of victims. Imagine also that the expected harm can be distributed in two different ways: either 10% to the discriminated group and 90% to the non-discriminated group, or vice versa. Imagine also that IRBs decrease the expected liability of the tortfeasor by 10%.[389] In the first scenario, the tortfeasor will expect to pay 99. Conversely, in the second scenario he will expect to pay 91. Thus, the deterrent capacity of tort law is lower in the second scenario than in the first one.

In addition, sometimes the variation in the deterrent effectiveness of tort law may depend directly on the composition of the population of victims. This occurs, for instance, when the expected harm is equally distributed among the population of victims. Imagine, for instance, a factory that discharges a certain amount of toxic wastes in an area inhabited by both members of the discriminated group and members of the non-discriminated group. This conduct increases the probability for the inhabitants of this area to contract a disease by 5% and the disease is likely to inflict a harm of 100 to each inhabitant of the area (independent of group membership). In this scenario, ceteris paribus, the greater the proportion of victims belonging to the discriminated group, the lower the expected liability of the tortfeasor.

This analysis suggests that in the Western world IRBs decrease the regulatory effectiveness of tort law in territorial areas inhabited by large communities of non-white individuals more than in white inhabited areas. For instance, the decrease in expected liability for a white polluter will be higher in Saint-Denis (one of the "black" banlieues of Paris), than in the 5th Arrondissement (one of the upper-class "white" neighborhoods of Paris). Indeed, there is evidence showing that members of discriminated groups tend to be more exposed to man-made environmental hazards.[390] While there are various factors that can explain these findings (e.g. housing

---

389 This number is put here as a mere example. To my knowledge, no study has quantified the decrease in expected liability given by racial biases, which could be either higher or lower than this number.

390 Mohai Paul, 2009. Environmental Justice, 34 ANNU. REV. ENVIRON. RESOUR, 405. On the role of tort law in environmental racism see: Bullard Robert and Beverly Wright, 2008. Disastrous

prices,[391] lower political power of ethnic minorities,[392] racism among regulators[393]), the present analysis suggests that IRBs might be one of them.

Note also that the higher exposure of minorities to harm from pollution need not to be necessarily the result of a conscious choice made by polluting entities (so-called targeting).[394] Conversely, a polluter may simply experience a different liability cost of his activity depending on the racial composition of the area in which he is located, which in turn may influence his choice to stay or relocate elsewhere.

The same occurs with regards to product liability. Here the larger is the proportion of consumers of a product that belongs to the discriminated group, the more IRBs are likely to decrease the expected liability of the manufacturer. For instance, this could be observed with regards to cosmetic products targeted to people of color or to food products that are largely consumed by members of discriminated groups. Similarly, IRBs will decrease more the deterrent capacity of tort law in sectors of the economy in which large proportions of victims are likely to be non-white. Such as in the agricultural sector in Italy, in which a large proportion of the workforce has non-European origins.[395]

4.5.4.2 IRBs and Deterrence When the Tortfeasor is a Member of a Discriminated Group

The previous section has analyzed the effect of IRBs in the judiciary, when the victim of a tort is a member of the discriminated group and it was concluded that the ability of tort law to deter undesirable activities might not independent of the racial group to which the tortfeasor and the victim belong. A similar conclusion is

---

Response to Natural and Man-Made Disasters: An Environmental Justice Analysis Twenty-Five Years after Warren County, 26 J. ENVTL. L. 217.

391 Hamilton James, 1995. Testing for Environmental Racism: Prejudice, Profits, Political Power? 14(1) J. POLICY ANAL. MANAG, 107.

392 Bullard Robert, 2000. Dumping in Dixie: Race, Class, and Environmental Quality Boulder, CO: WESTVIEW PRESS; David Pellow, 2002. Garbage Wars: The Struggle For Environmental Justice In Chicago, MIT PRESS.

393 Laura Pulido, 2000. Rethinking Environmental Racism: White Privilege and Urban Development in Southern California. 90(1) ANN. AM. ASSOC. GEOGR 12.

394 On the targeting racial minorities by polluting companies in the US see Chapter 5.

395 For a recent study on the employment of immigrants in the Italian agricultural sector see: INEA, 2012. Indagine sull'Impiego degli Immigrati in Agricoltura in Italia.

reached with regards to the situation in which the tortfeasor is a member of the discriminated group.

In particular, as above, when the victim is a member of the discriminated group, the expected liability of the tortfeasor is lower than in absence of the bias. This also implies that when the victim of the tort is a member of the non-discriminated group, the expected liability of the tortfeasor might increase. In addition, because of IRBs, this expected liability might be higher when the tortfeasor is a member of a discriminated group than otherwise. As explained above, this could be due to the fact that direct harm is not independent from the ability of the adversary to effectively convince the judge of the truthfulness of the version of the facts that is more favorable to him. When the victim belongs to the same racial group of the judge, the tortfeasor is in a position of even greater disadvantage than if she belonged to the non-discriminated group.

This implies that for every possible composition of the population of victims in terms of proportion of members of the non-discriminated and discriminated group, ceteris paribus, the expected liability of the tortfeasor member of the discriminated group might be higher than the one of the member of the non-discriminated group. This can have significant consequences for the wellbeing of members of discriminated groups. In addition, this can have a broader impact on the wellbeing of the society as a whole. For instance, when in absence of the bias judges correctly apply the marginal Hand formula, the bias may decrease social welfare. To illustrate what I discussed in this paragraph, let's consider Figure 2. below.

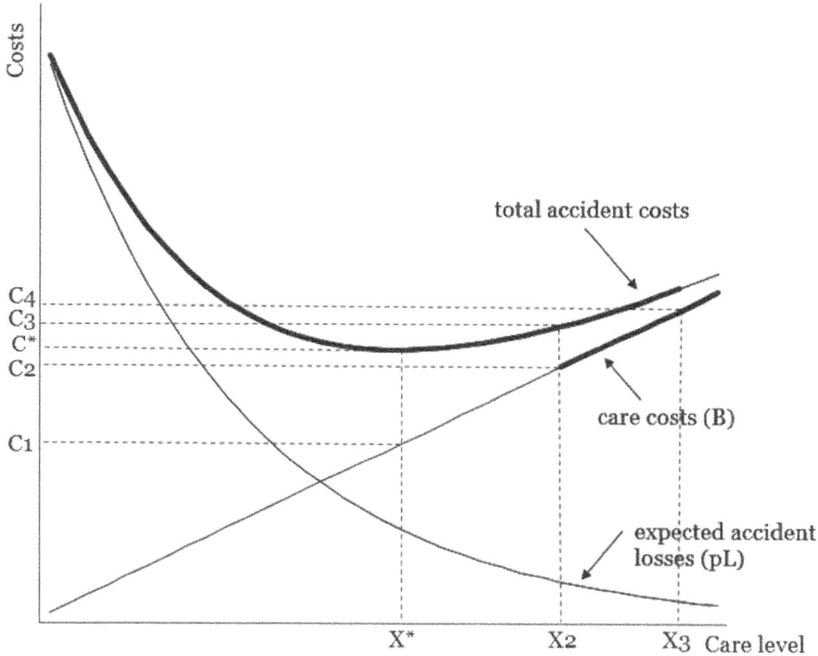

Figure 2 The effect of IRBs on social cost when the tortfeasor is a member of a discriminated group.

If in absence of IRBs judges correctly apply the marginal Hand formula to determine negligence, tortfeasors have an incentive to take the level of precautions X*, which is also the one that minimizes the social cost of accidents (C*). However, when due to IRBs judges require minority members to take a level of precautions equal to X2, the latter will have an incentive to adapt to this level of care to avoid paying also for the losses suffered by victims. As shown in the graph, care costs at X2 are higher than at X*, and therefore IRBs disadvantage minority members. In addition, the social cost of accidents is higher at X2 than at X*. This inefficient incentive disappears at higher levels of due care. For instance, when biased judges increase the due care level to X3, the tortfeasor prefers to invest in a care level of X* and bear the whole social cost of accidents instead of investing in precautionary measures at the C4 level. While this does not decrease social welfare, it redistributes resources from tortfeasors to victims because in this situation the tortfeaosor bears also the expected accident losses.

In addition, when the tortfeasor is an entrepreneur or a self-employed person, the effect of IRBs in the judiciary would be to create an uneven playing field between enterprises run by members of different racial groups, thus reducing competition in the market. Indeed, evidence indicates that non-white entrepreneurs face more difficulties than their white competitors in running their business in the EU.[396] While several factors may account for these results, the analysis proposed here suggests that IRBs in the judiciary may contribute to worsen an already uneasy situation.

4.5.5 Stereotypes and Deterrence

In the previous section, it has been argued that IRBs in the judiciary might decrease the ability of tort law to optimally deter tortfeasors when the victims of the tort are members of discriminated groups. Here, I shall defend this conclusion against possible critique concerning the accuracy of stereotypes and the importance of accuracy in courts' adjudication for the achievement of deterrence and social welfare maximization.

4.5.5.1 On the (In)Accuracy of Stereotypes

As discussed above, law and economics scholarship suggests that accuracy in courts' adjudication is a major factor influencing deterrence.[397] Higher degrees of accuracy in adjudication lead to more deterrence because, generally, tortfeasors' decisions to engage in an harmful activity become more expensive when courts correctly establish liability at trial (unless inaccuracy leads to excessive liability).[398] In addition, inaccuracy in the establishment of liability makes the choice of not engaging in the harmful activity more expensive.[399] If implicit stereotypes increased courts' accuracy in assessing facts at trial, one could argue

396 On issues related to the development of entrepreneurship among members of ethnic minorities in Europe see: OECD-European Union, 2013. The Missing Entrepreneurs: Policies for Inclusive Entrepreneurship in Europe, OECD PUBLISHING.

397 Richard Posner, 1973. An Economic Approach to Legal Procedure and Judicial Administration, 2 J. LEG. STUD 339; Louis Kaplow, 1994. The Value of Accuracy in Adjudication: An Economic Analysis, 23(1) The J. LEG. STUD, 348; Garoupa Nuno and Matteo Rizzolli, 2012. Wrongful Convictions Do Lower Deterrence, 168(2) JITE, 224.

398 Kaplow (1994).

399 Ibid.

that IRBs can increase the deterrent capacity of tort law. In this section, I argue that this conclusion may not hold.[400]

Psychologists have long debated the issue of stereotype accuracy,[401] and the discussion has more recently moved to the realm of implicit racial stereotypes in legal settings.[402] Some commentators have argued that implicit racial stereotypes may actually be accurate in the sense that they may have predictive value.[403] The alleged accuracy of these stereotypes would be the result of people's observation of empirical realities that would be translated into mental models subsequently used to understand reality.[404] Proponents of the inclusion of the results obtained in the literature on IRBs in policy-making do not deny the existence of this possibility.[405] However, several authors have highlighted various reasons for which it may not be the case that implicit stereotypes increase the accuracy of a judgment.

Kang offers various arguments to support the inaccuracy of implicit stereotypes.[406] First, he argues that information regarding racial stereotypes is mainly provided indirectly, through mass media, education and experiences reported by others. Since it reflects popular culture, this information is unlikely to be highly accurate.[407] Recent findings have confirmed that both explicit stereotypical consistent information and more subtle information (nonverbal language) provided through television is able to influence implicit stereotypes against racial minorities.[408] The observed human tendency to prefer sharing stereotypical consistent

---

400 To be clear, I am not suggesting that if IRBs increased courts' ability to deter tortfeasors we should not try to eradicate these biases from the courtroom. Indeed, there are other reasons to counteract these biases.

401 See: Judd Charles and Bernadette Park, 1993. Definition and Assessment of Accuracy in Social Stereotypes, 100(1) PSYCHOL. REV 109; Jussim Lee et al. 2009. The Unbearable Accuracy of Stereotypes, Handbook of Prejudice, Stereotyping and Discrimination, (T.D. Nelson Eds.), TAYLOR AND FRANCIS, 199.

402 See: Greenwald and Krieger (2006); Mitchell and Tetlock, (2006); Kang, (2010).

403 Mitchell and Tetlock (2006).

404 Ibid.

405 Greenwald and Krieger (2006).

406 Kang (2010).

407 Kang (2010).

408 Weisbuch Max et al., 2009. The Subtle Transmission of Race Bias Via Televised Nonverbal Behavior, 326 SCIENCE, 1711; Arendt Florian and Temple Northup, 2015. Effects of Long-Term Exposure to News Stereotypes on Implicit and Explicit Attitudes, 9 INT. J. COMMUN, 2370.

information over stereotypical inconsistent information adds to the list of reasons why we may be skeptical of the accuracy of implicit stereotypes.[409]

Second, evidence indicates that individuals tend to see illusory correlations between two events when these events are salient, such as a minority member and a negative event.[410] This, in turn, leads to overestimating the frequency by which these events occur together.[411]

Third, there is some evidence suggesting that we tend to recall information in a manner that is consistent with the stereotypes we hold.[412] In addition, Kang highlights that empirical evidence suggests that, for motivational reasons, humans tend to exaggerate positive traits of in-groups and negative traits of outgroup.[413] Last, various studies suggest that we tend to exaggerate the homogeneity of outgroup members.[414]

These arguments support the claim that stereotypical accuracy in the domain of implicit biases may not be very high. Note that accuracy is almost always a matter of degrees. Thus, for implicit stereotypes to increase deterrence, it would not suffice for them to be somewhat accurate. Conversely, they would need to be accurate to a degree that increases the accuracy of courts' decisions.

4.5.5.2 Beyond Accuracy: Implicit Stereotypes and the Economics of Character Evidence

Implicit stereotypes are, to a certain extent, similar to character evidence. As character evidence, they lead the adjudicator to believe that a certain individual has a higher/lower propensity to engage in certain conducts (depending on whether she is identified as belonging to a certain racial group or another). When seen through these lenses, it appears that even a perfectly accurate implicit stereotype may lead to decreases in social welfare. Below, I will formulate this argument by referring to the law and economics literature on the use of character evidence.

---

409 For a review of this literature see: Kashima Yoshihisa et al., 2007. Grounding: Sharing Information in Social Interaction, in Social Communication, (Klaus Fiedler Eds.), PSYCHOLOGY PRESS.

410 Kang (2010).

411 Kang (2010).

412 Kang (2010); Levinson (2007).

413 Kang (2010). On the Outgroup Homogeneity Bias see below.

414 Kang (2010).

Traditionally, the economic argument on the ban on character evidence has been in line with the discussion on character evidence and accuracy. From this perspective, whether character evidence should be admitted at trial, ultimately depends on whether it increases accuracy in fact-finding.[415] However, Sanchirico has more recently highlighted that the problems related to the use of character evidence and deterrence may go beyond the accuracy issue.[416] In fact, the problem lies also in the predictive nature of character evidence. In this connection, predictive evidence refers to items of evidence that exist regardless of whether the act under scrutiny at trial has been committed or not.[417] This type of evidence is usually distinguished from trace evidence, meaning any item of evidence that tends to be created by the tortious conduct object of the trial,[418] such as the testimony of a witness regarding the speed of an alleged tortfeasor in a car accident case. If the object of the trial is identified in welfare maximization vis-à-vis accuracy, the distinction between trace and predictive evidence becomes of particular importance because tort law generally applies to unwarranted consequences of otherwise beneficial behavior. In this connection, propensity evidence can be seen as a sign that the alleged tortfeasor derives a greater benefit from engaging in the conduct object of the trial than the individual for which such evidence could not be gathered. As long as the individual internalizes the cost of her activity, she will receive incentives to behave in a socially welfare maximizing manner.[419] Any attempt to deter her more because of her character, would result in a decrease in social welfare.[420]

Bridging these insights on character evidence with the debate on the accuracy of implicit stereotypes highlights that even if judges were relying on a perfectly accurate implicit stereotype, social welfare could be decreased compared to a state of the world in which implicit stereotypes did not affect courts' decisions. Indeed, to the extent that a stereotype mirrors a higher propensity of members of a racial group to engage in an activity, one may infer that the stereotype captures the preferences of the members of that group.

---

415 See above for a debate on this issue.

416 Chris Sanchirico, 2001. Character Evidence and the Object of Trial. COLUMBIA LAW REV. 1227.

417 Uviller Richard, Evidence of Character to Prove Conduct: Illusion, Logic, and Justice in the Courtroom, 130 UNIV. PA. LAW REV 847.

418 Ibid.

419 Sanchirico (2001).

420 Ibid.

Thus, Sanchirico's perspective on character evidence leads to a different conclusion from the discussion on the accuracy implicit stereotypes and deterrence. In particular, when seen through these lenses, implicit stereotypes may decrease social welfare even when they increase the accuracy of adjudication.

4.5.5.3 Beyond Accuracy: Other Relevant Aspects

The conclusion reached in Section 4.4 does not rely solely on the arguments that implicit stereotypes decrease the accuracy of courts' decisions and that IRBs act as forms of character evidence. Two other reasons support the abovementioned conclusion.

First, as discussed above, the mere belief of being discriminated against imposes a cost on members of discriminated groups that want to bring a case to trial, thus reducing the expected liability of the tortfeasor. This cost is not necessarily attenuated by the high accuracy of implicit stereotypes. This is because, even assuming that members of discriminated groups know about the increase in accuracy of courts' decisions, it is not necessarily true that believing of being discriminated against hurts less when discrimination increases courts' accuracy at trial.[421] This implies that even when implicit stereotypes increase courts' accuracy, they might not increase tort deterrence.

Second, note also that implicit stereotypes account only for a fraction of direct harm and signalling, being the remaining part a result of implicit attitudes. Contrary to stereotypes, implicit attitudes are not evaluable in terms of accuracy.[422] This implies that even if implicit stereotypes were able to increase courts' accuracy at trial, they would account only for a fraction of the effect of IRBs on tort deterrence and would therefore not necessarily overturn the finding that IRBs reduce the capacity of tort law to deter undesirable activities.

It is important to highlight that to the extent that IRBs decrease courts' accuracy, the deterrent capacity of tort law might be undermined beyond what suggested by the analysis proposed above.

---

421 Whether this is the case is an empirical question that goes beyond the scope of the present work. To the best of my knowledge, no study has inquired this issue empirically.

422 Kang (2010).

4.5.6 Implicit Racial Biases in the Cathedral: Issues of Optimal Deterrence

In the previous two sections it was concluded that the deterrent effectiveness of tort law might be a function of the racial group to which the tortfeasor, the victim and the judge belong. Tort law is, however, only one of the possible legal tools that could be used to deter undesired activities. Law and economics shows that both Pigovian taxes and regulation can, at least partially, substitute liability law in this endeavour. The analysis proposed in this work highlights that the optimal combination of these various instruments is not necessarily independent from the racial composition of judiciaries, population of victims and population of tortfeasors.

Note that the issue of whether IRBs suggest a broader use of taxation and/or regulation is not only of interests for law and economics scholars, but also for legal scholars more in general. Indeed, whether regulation or taxation could effectively reduce the necessity to rely on an unjust tort law system to prevent accidents is a non-trivial question to be addressed.

4.6 Policy Responses

The previous Section has illustrated that IRBs in tort trials are likely to decrease social welfare. In light of this, it can be interesting to discuss which policies could be implemented to reduce the effect of these biases on trial outcomes. I will start by discussing remedies aimed at tackling the effect of IRBs on trial outcomes. Subsequently, I highlight some of the limits of this approach and other potential policy pathways.

4.6.1 Debiasing and Insulating Implicit Biases

Behavioral scientists generally distinguish between two types of strategies that could be implemented to prevent biases in decision-making: debiasing and insulating. Insulation refers to legal techniques that foreclose the possibility for an individual to make biased decisions.[423] Conversely, as mentioned above, debiasing improves the decisionmaking of the individual without preventing him to make a decision.[424] I shall follow this distinction in discussing this subject matter.

423 Christine and Sunstein (2006).

424 Ibid.

Debiasing can take various forms in the context of judicial decision-making. In this connection, psychological research indicates that making a person accountable can decrease the influence of implicit racial biases on judgment.[425] Legal systems have a plethora of options to create accountability in the courtroom. For instance, requiring judges to motivate and publish their decisions, the appeal system as well as the publicity of the trial are all institutional and procedural features that make judges accountable for their choice. These features are generally already well present in European tort trials. Yet, it is important to stress that legal systems can vary in terms of the strength of accountability mechanisms put in place. For instance, the decision style employed by the French Court de Cassation (Court of Cassation), characterized by short and not necessarily transparent motivations, may be less effective in inducing judges to feel accountable compared to, for instance, the relatively longer motivations usually written by the Italian Corte di Cassazione (Court of Cassation). Of course, shorter motivations can have some advantage over longer ones, as they make, for example, the trial faster. Thus, my argument is not that, because of implicit biases, we necessarily should require courts to write long decisions. Conversely, my, more mild, claim is that the literature on implicit biases suggests that there might be gains from employing stronger (and maybe more costly) accountability mechanisms.

Besides accountability, two other structural interventions that could decrease racially biased decision-making relate to time and diversity in the courtroom. In terms of time, since implicit biases are the product of automatic mental processes which are particularly likely to affect human decision-making in situations in which thorough deliberation is limited, providing judges with sufficient time to decide a case may help avoiding racial biases.[426] This is an aspect that should be taken into account when discussing policies aimed to speed up the functioning of tort law systems.

On the diversity side of the coin, psychological research indicates that exposure to positive examples of members of discriminated groups may help reducing implicit biases.[427] Various authors have therefore highlighted the importance of guaranteeing diversity in the judiciary.[428] Increasing diversity in European judicia-

---

425 Kang et al. (2012).

426 Kang et al. (2012).

427 Kang et al. (2012).

428 Kang et al. (2012); Smith and Levinson (2012).

ries may not be an easily implementable policy, also from a political point of view. In this connection, an alternative - and more easily implementable - measure is to introduce images of positive examples of member of racial minorities in the working environment of judges (e.g. on the walls or as screensavers).[429] Yet, it is still highly debated whether such debiasing strategy has long term effects in the real world. In particular, Rachlinski and co-authors have found no statistically significant differences in the biases held by judges coming from court districts with significantly differences in magistrates racial composition.[430] Further research in this direction is therefore needed.

On the insulating side of the coin, a strategy that is sometimes already in place in several European tort systems concerns preventing judges from making decisions in situations of high ambiguity. As discussed above, implicit biases affect decision-making more easily when a person faces ambiguous information. In trial settings the degree of ambiguity is often linked to the norm enforced by the court. In this regard, tort law is a relatively dynamic area of the law in which vague unwritten norms have to be concretized ex post by the court in the individual case. The court often has leeway in determining, for instance, whether the defendant acted unlawfully and what the due care standard for particular conduct is. This ambiguity is not always present in other areas of the law. In criminal law, for example, due to the principle of *nulla poena sine lege*, ex ante it is more clear which behaviors constitute crimes. These differences suggest that even though most literature on IRBs focuses on criminal law, this is not necessarily the area of the law in which IRBs have the largest societal effects. A reduction of this ambiguity in tort law settings can be achieved when a more concrete tort/negligence standard is established via legislation/regulation. Thus, by directly intervening in shaping tort law rules, the legislator could insulate the judge from making decisions in situations of high ambiguity. To a lesser extent, a similar effect could be achieved over time, via precedents, by judge made law.

429 Kang et al. (2012).

430 Rachlinski et al. (2009).

4.6.2 Looking Beyond Behavioral Strategies: Traditional Instruments to Solve a New Problem?

The previous Section has highlighted various policies that could reduce the effect of IRBs on trial outcomes. This Section discusses two limits of these interventions and a possible alternative path to address issues arising from the effect of IRBs on trial outcomes.

A first limit of the interventions highlighted in the previous Section is that, as shown in Section 4, the effect of implicit racial biases on courts' decisions can occur through the creation of evidence outside the trial. This implies that any measure that aims to tackle the issue of implicit racial biases directly in the courtroom alone may not eradicate the problem of discrimination at trial. Second, a failure to recognize the role of biased pre-constituted evidence, can greatly hinder the effective and efficient intervention on the effect of implicit racial biases on trial outcomes.

To illustrate, imagine a society in which a limited amount of resources can be allocated to the prevention of implicit racial biases. Imagine also that in this society the impact of implicit racial biases on trial outcomes is determined 20% by courts' perception and evaluation of evidence (Factor 1) and 80% by items of evidence created outside the trial (Factor 2). The resources can be allocated only to one of the two factors, and they will reduce the impact of the selected factor by 10%. In this case, deciding to act directly on courts' perception and evaluation of evidence would neither be the most effective nor the most efficient way of dealing with the problem.

My contention here is not that policies aimed at reducing the impact of implicit racial biases in the courtroom are necessarily not effective/efficient or not worth pursuing. My point is that we should not miss the broader picture of the actual way in which trial outcomes are determined. Going back to the example above, which of the two aforementioned policies would be more effective/efficient may depends on various factors, such as: the situations in which implicit racial biases are more likely to affect human decision-making;[431] the degree by which

---

431 For an analysis of the situational factors that increase the influence of implicit racial biases in the courtroom see for instance: NCSC, Helping Courts Address Implicit Bias: Strategies to Reduce the Influence of Implicit Bias, available at: http://www.ncsc.org.

courts rely on pre-constituted evidence to decide cases;[432] the ethnic composition of judiciaries and medical staff (e.g. with regards to the effect of the bias on the determination of pain and suffering)[433]; the use of group decision-making to create items of evidence within and outside the trial; etc. Determining which of the two options is the best is not an easy task, but more research in this direction could provide some insight for a more informed policymaking.[434]

A possible pathway to address these issues is to explore the possibility of using alternative legal regimes to reduce the influence of implicit racial biases in the society. Economic analysis of law coupled with psychology allows comparing the effect of implicit racial biases on different substitutable legal tools and consider whether to opt for a different combination of them. The availability of tax law and regulation implies that tort law is only one of the instruments that can be used to prevent accidents. In this perspective, if taxation and/or regulation were found to be immune from, or at least less affected by, implicit racial biases, they could be seen as special forms of insulating strategies that prevent biased judges from making biased decisions by reducing society's reliance on tort law to regulate certain activities. In this connection, while it is not clear whether regulation (and it's enforcement by governmental authorities) are necessarily less biased than judges, Pigouvian taxes with their uniform application to polluting entities might be a relatively less affected by implicit biases than tort law.

4.7 Conclusions

This Chapter contributes to the ongoing legal debate on IRBs by focusing on European tort trials. I analyze of how IRBs can affect the creation, presentation, and evaluation of evidence in tort trials. Overall, the study suggests that IRBs may affect courts' decisions in several stages of a trial in relation to all the main elements of tort law (losses, causation and negligence). My study also highlights that IRBs can reduce social welfare by altering the deterrent capacity of tort law.

432 The role of pre-constituted evidence in determining trial outcomes varies from legal system to legal system.

433 In this regard, recall that black individuals tend, on average, to have less strong implicit preferences than white individuals.

434 The previous section was focused on implicit racial biases and tort law trials, however, this argument would equally apply also to other contexts (such as criminal cases), in which part of the evidence used at trial is produced outside the courtroom.

This can occur also in situations in which implicit biases improve the accuracy of judicial decisions. Lastly, I discuss various policies (and their limits) that could be put in place to reduce these unwarranted effects. In this respect, the analysis shows that some remedies are available and some of these are already put in place in the context of tort law trials in some European countries. The analysis, however, highlights also that the effectiveness and efficiency of these interventions is often still unknown.

5 Gender and Race-Based Statistical Tables in European Tort Trials[435]

5.1 Introduction

The previous Chapter has analyzed the issue of racial discrimination at trial by looking at the role of IRBs. This Chapter expands the analysis of the behavioral law and economics of discrimination at trial by looking at the role of race and gender based statistical tables. In relation to accuracy, this Chapter refers to the law and economics of accuracy in damages assessments in tort law.

The use of gender and race-based statistical tables (e.g. life expectancy; work-life expectancy and average wage tables) for the estimation of damages for future losses in US tort law has long been studied by legal scholars.[436] Traditionally, this scholarship has criticized this practice from the perspective of distributive justice. A recent concern raised by this literature is that the use of non-blended tables, i.e. tables that report data distinguishing between gender and racial lines, may lead to

---

[435] This Chapter is partially a reproduction of the article: Goran Dominioni, 2017. Biased Damages Awards: Gender and Race Discrimination in Tort Trials, 1 INT'L COMP., POLICY & ETHICS L. REV. 269. I am grateful to Stephen Billion, Ignacio Cofone, Pieter Desmet, Michael Faure, Klaus Heine, Elena Kantorowicz-Reznichenko, Joe Rieff, Alessandro Romano, Alan Schwartz, Louis Visscher and the participants to the Rotterdam Institute of Law and Economics and the Erasmus Graduate School of Law seminars for useful discussion. I gratefully acknowledge financial support from Behavioral Approaches to Contracts and Torts (BACT) research program and Erasmus Trusfonds.

[436] Jennifer Wriggins, 2007. Damages in Tort Litigation: Thoughts on Race and Remedies, 1865–2007, 27 REVIEW OF LITIG. 37; Martha Chamallas and Jennifer Wriggins, 2010. The Measure of Injury: Race, Gender, and Tort Law, NYU PRESS; Laura Greenberg, 2001. Comment, Compensating the Lead Poisoned Child: Proposals for Mitigating Discriminatory Damage Awards, 28 B.C. ENVTL. AFF. L. REV. 429; Martha Chamallas, 1998. The Architecture of Bias: Deep Structures in Tort Law, 146 U. PA. L. REV. 463; Sherri Lamb, 1996. Toward Gender-Neutral Data for Adjudicating Lost Future Earning Damages: An Evidentiary Perspective, 72 CHI. KENT L. REV. 299; see also Elaine Gibson, 1993. The Gendered Wage Dilemma in Personal Injury Damages, in TORT THEORY 185, (Ken Cooper-Stephenson & Elaine Gibson eds.); Ken Cooper–Stephenson, 1979. Damages for Loss of Working Capacity for Women, 43 SASKATCHEWAN L. REV. 7; Ronen Avraham and Kimberly Yuracko, 2017. Torts and Discrimination, 78(3) OHIO ST. L. J. 661.

G. Dominioni, *Biased Trials*, Ökonomische Analyse des Rechts | Economic Analysis of Law, https://doi.org/10.1007/978-3-658-30080-7_5

targeting of women and members of racial minorities.[437] The targeting effect may per se perpetuate and worsen existing inequalities among gender and racial groups, thus making the use of non-blended tables even less warranted from a distributive justice standpoint.[438] Yet, traditionally tort law scholars adhering to the corrective justice and welfare maximization schools of thought have supported this practice. Starting from these premises a recent paper by Avraham and Yuracko has put forward various arguments to show that the use of non-blended tables is not warranted for the achievement of corrective justice and efficiency.[439] In this connection, despite the debate on the use of non-blended tables has developed mainly in the US, this issue is of clear relevance also for European tort law. Indeed, this is an issue that in recent years has received considerable attention in several European countries.[440] The present work contributes to this literature in two ways.

First, it provides a comparative analysis on the employment of non-blended tables in the US, England, France, and Italy. These last three are major traditions in European tort law and thus the analysis can provide some insight on how European courts deal with this issue. This analysis complements the legal scholarship in the related field of insurance law that, in recent years, has given substantial attention to the use of gender-based insurance premium pricing.[441] Especially after the ECJ decision that has found this practice to be inconsistent with the unisex price principle established by the EU legislation on equality between genders.[442]

Second, it analyzes the welfare effects of the two approaches (blended vs non-blended tables) from a behavioral law and economics standpoint.

The main findings of this Chapter are the following. First, with some exception, gender and race-based tables have a minor role in the establishment of damages in England, France, and Italy. Thus, on the basis of this analysis, courts' practice regarding the employment of non-blended tables seems to be of less controversial nature in the Old continent than in the US. Second, taking a behavioral

437 Avraham and Yuracko (2017). In this context, targeting refers to the redirection of unintentionally created expected harm. In other words, this term identifies losses imposed as a by-product of an otherwise socially beneficial activity.

438 Avraham and Yuracko (2017).

439 Ibid.

440 See, for instance, the judicial debate that took place recently in both Italy and England (below).

441 See, for instance: Tobler Christa, 2011. Case C-236/09, Association belge des Consommateurs Test-Achats ASBL, Yann van Vurgt, Charles Basselier v. Conseil des ministres. 48 COMMON MARK. LAW REV 2041.

442 Test-Achats case (C-236/09).

perspective on this issue highlights that the welfarist case for this practice is weaker than previously thought. This is because a behavioral approach to the issue strengthens many of the arguments put forward by Avraham and Yuracko. In this sense, the present work complements and supports their recent claim that law and economics scholarship should back the use of blended tables.

The remaining part of the Chapter unfolds as follows: Section 2 discusses the role of accuracy in the determination of damages at trial. Secion 3 describes the link between the employment of non-blended tables and targeting. Section 4 provides a comparative analysis of the use of gender and race-based tables in the US, England, France and Italy. Section 5 discusses the arguments in favor of and against this practice from a neoclassical law and economics perspective. Section 6 assesses the welfare effects of this practice via the lenses of behavioral law and economics. Section 7 concludes.

5.2 The Economics of Accuracy in the Determination of Damages

Many of the economic arguments in favor and against the use of blended tables relate to how accurate these tables are. This section introduces the economics of accuracy in the determination of damages to set the ground for the discussion that will follow.

Law and economics scholarship has long explored the role of accuracy in the determination of damages in tort trials for the creation of social welfare.[443] A main result in this literature is that accuracy is generally an important element of a well-functioning tort law system, but that various caveats apply to this general finding.[444]

The first caveat refers to whether inaccuracies in adjudication are systematic or not.[445] The behavioral incentives provided by tort law to tortfeasors to invest in precautionary measures and reduce the activity level, operate ex-ante, i.e. before the accident takes place.[446] From an ex-ante perspective, the injurer can adjust her conduct to the incentives only based on the damages that she expects to pay from

443 Louis Kaplow and Steven Shavell, 1996. Accuracy in the Assessment of Damages. 39(1) J. LAW ECON 191.

444 Kaplow and Shavell (1996).

445 Ibid.

446 As above, for simplicity I will discuss here only the behavioural incentives to tortfeasors, i.e. the behavioural incentives needed in unilateral accidents.

engaging in a certain activity. From this it follows that an ex-post increase in the accuracy of damages awarded does not necessarily improve the quality of the incentives set by tort law. Generally, as long as the average of damages awarded corresponds to the actual average loss suffered by victims, the behavioral incentives will be appropriate.[447] Conversely, a systematic discrepancy between these two averages may reduce social welfare. In particular, a systematic underestimation of the losses suffered by victims will send a too low price signal to the tortfeasor, potentially inducing her to invest too little in precautionary measures and engage too much in the activity.[448] A mirror image situation occurs when damages awarded systematically overestimate the actual losses suffered by victims.[449] Here the tortfeasor would receive too high incentives to invest in precautionary measures and to reduce her activity level. Thus, only systematic departures from the average loss caused by tortious activities can matter for deterrence.[450]

A second caveat that limits the welfare benefits of accuracy in adjudication are the costs related to accuracy.[451] In particular, to increase accuracy in adjudication additional information is often needed. Obtaining, processing and storing this information can be costly and for this reason not every increase in accuracy brings a society closer to greater welfare. It is for this reason that damages are often established in abstract.[452] An example of a determination of damages that is often carried out at an abstract level relates to material harm to cars.[453] Here, for instance, the damage is often assessed by considering the cost that a mechanic would charge to repair the car, regardless of whether the reparation actually takes place.[454]

Having briefly discussed the economics of accuracy in determination of damages in tort trial, the next section discusses targeting incentives that may arise from the use of non-blended tables.

---

447 Kaplow and Shavell (1996).

448 Ibid.

449 Ibid.

450 Ibid.

451 Ibid.

452 Michael Faure and Louis Visscher, 2011. The Role of Experts in Assessing Damages–A Law and Economics Account. 2(3) EUROPEAN JOURNAL OF RISK REGULATION 379.

453 Ibid.

454 Ibid.

5.3 Race and Gender-Based Statistical Tables and Targeting

Governmental authorities in most Western countries gather population data related to: i) life expectancy, namely the average residual number of years that a person at a certain age is expected to live; ii) work-life expectancy, i.e. the average residual number of years that a person at a certain age is expected to work; iii) average wage. These data are organized in tables and made available to the public. Courts often rely on these tables to estimate various types of damages in tort trials.[455] For instance, life-expectancy tables are often used to estimate the future medical costs of treatments that a victim of a tort has to endure throughout the course of her life as a consequence of the accident. Similarly, work-life expectancy tables can be used to estimate the future losses of earning capacity.

As highlighted in the literature, the use of gender and race-based statistical tables (i.e. statistical tables that differentiate between male and female and between members of different racial groups) can lead to targeting of specific racial and gender groups.[456] Indeed, as long as the social cost of a particular activity is established according to these tables and this cost is further reflected in the due care standard and/or the damages awards set by courts, the private costs of the tortfeasor will vary depending on social group harmed by the activity.

Let us start with the analysis of targeting in relation to the standard of negligence. From a law and economics perspective, under a negligence rule courts should set the due care standard on the basis of the (marginal) Hand formula.[457] Within this framework, the higher the expected harm of an activity, the more precautions the tortfeasor has to take in order to escape liability. Thus, to the extent that tortfeasors are able to predict the racial or gender group of the potential victims of their activity, economic theory suggests that they receive incentives to target the social group that is less costly to harm. For instance, imagine that a company has two factories that produce the same good. One factory is located in a neighborhood inhabited predominantly by Black people and the other is located in

455 See below for a discussion of the use of these tables in various Western countries.

456 Avraham and Yuracko (2017).

457 For a discussion of whether and to what extent European courts indeed establish the due care standard according to the Hand formula see: Heico Kerkmeester and Louis Visscher, 2003. Learned Hand in Europe: A Study in the Comparative Law and Economics of Negligence, GERMAN WORKING PAPERS IN LAW AND ECONOMICS 6. Jef De Moot et al., 2004. The Learned Hand Formula: The Case of the Netherlands, 4(2) GLOBAL JURIST ADVANCES.

a predominantly White area. Imagine also that both factories need maintenance in order to reduce the probability of industrial disasters to occur. Yet, the company has a limited budget that allows maintenance work only in one of the two factories. If the average income of Whites is higher than income of Blacks and loss of income is a foreseeable loss, harming a White person is ceteris paribus more expensive. In this situation, the polluting company receives an incentive to invest in maintenance in the factory located in the neighborhood inhabited by White people. This is because, under a strict application of the marginal Hand formula, the due care standard is lower when the victim is a Black person than when it is a White person.

In addition, and maybe more importantly given that a strict application of the marginal Hand formula seems not to be common in contemporary European tort law,[458] this incentive to targeting will be present also when courts fix the due care standard without considering the social cost imposed by an activity. To understand why this is the case, imagine that courts were imposing the same standard of care to all conducts (e.g. maintenance of factories' equipment) occurring in a certain area. Even in this case, if tortfeasors are sometimes asked to compensate the victim (either because their actual or perceived care level was lower than the due care standard), their expected liability is lower when they target the social group that is cheaper to harm.

The large literature on environmental racism provide a clear example in which targeting might be at play.[459] As explained in above, environmental racism refers to the phenomenon by which member of racial minorities are disproportionally exposed more to environmental hazards than members of non-racial minorities.[460] Clearly there are various political, economic, and ideological factors that can account for this phenomenon. Yet, as it is argued in the following, the lower cost of harming minority members is not necessarily a negligible one.[461] Besides environmental racism, these dynamics can occur also in other settings where racial

458 Kerkmeester and Visscher (2003).

459 Avraham and Yuracko (2017).

460 Mohai et al. (2009).

461 Avraham and Yuracko (2017); Bullard and Wright, 2008. Disastrous Response to Natural and Man-Made Disasters: An Environmental Justice Analysis Twenty-Five Years after Warren County, 26 J. ENVIRON. LAW, 217.

disparities in exposure to harm have been documented, such as medical malpractice and lead paint.[462] Similarly, as highlighted above with regards to the effect of IRBs on the functioning of tort law systems, trends of this type might be observed in the context of product liability when certain products are marketed to a specific social group identified by race or, given the broader scope of the present Chapter, gender. Companies are indeed often able to predict with a certain degree of accuracy whether a particular product will be marketed prominently to males or females. Research indicates that, it is sufficient to change the color of a product or other details related to the packaging to shift the consumption of a product from one gender group to another.[463]

Note that given the current gaps in socioeconomic status (SES) across gender and racial groups in many Western societies,[464] the differences in damages awarded are not necessarily trivial. Thus, targeting incentives might be non-negligible. For instance, according to the US Census Bureau, in 2015 the average yearly income of a White male was 60,448 dollars which was considerably higher than the average yearly income of a Black male (38,846 dollars) as well as of a White female (36,275 dollars) and a Black female (30,710 dollars) in the same year.[465] Imagine that a judge is called to assess the loss of future earning capacity of a Black and a White two years old child on the basis of these tables. Even ignoring potential differences in terms of work-life expectancy (which in reality is lower for Black people and for Women compared to White men),[466] by multiplying the abovementioned sums for a work-life expectancy of 35 years, the resulting damages awards would be respectively of: 2,115,680 (White male); 1,359,610 (Black male); 1,269,625 (White female); 1,074,850 (Black female). These differences can be non-trivial in terms of the incentives that they provide to potential tortfeasors. Indeed, in this example, shifting the externality from a White man to a Black woman can reduce the expected liability of a tortfeasor by about 50%.

---

462 Avraham and Yuracko (2017).

463 Auster Carol and Claire Mansbach, 2012. The Gender Marketing of Toys: An Analysis of Color And Type Of Toy On The Disney Store Website. 67(7) SEX ROLES, 375.

464 See for instance, Goran Dominioni et al., 2018. A Mathematical Approach to Study and Forecast Racial Groups Interactions: Deterministic Modeling and Scenario Method, 52(4) QUAL. QUANT 1929.

465 See: Table P-3. Race and Hispanic Origin of People by Mean Income and Sex, available at: http://www.census.gov/data/tables/time-series/demo/income-poverty/historical-income-people.html

466 Avraham and Yuracko, 2017.

An assumption underlying this reasoning is that tort law has actually a deterrent effect. This is indeed a debated issue among scholars. While economic modelling provides compelling reasons why we should expect tort law to have a deterrent effect, various authors are skeptic of the predictive validity of these results. In particular, it has been argued that many accidents are the product of momentary lapses in attention, that can not be avoided by the imposition of liability.[467] Against this claims, empirical evidence from the field provides some support to the economic intuition in the field of product liability and car accidents.[468] This, suggests that, at the margin, the use of non-blended tables can provide targeting incentives.

It is important to stress that targeting is not necessarily the result of the employment of race and gender-based statistical tables. Indeed, even if these tables were not employed and damages awards were based solely on the current income of the victim, it could still be cheaper for a tortfeasor to harm members of a particular racial or gender group. Yet, the use of statistical tables is often identified in the literature as a factor that leads to further discrepancies in the award of damages (and potentially the setting of the due care standard) across racial and gender groups.[469] This is because the employment of these tables expands differences in damages awards along racial and gender lines to situations in which the current situation of the victim would not suggest to do so (e.g. when the victim is an infant). In addition, the use of these tables is controversial also in light of the potential flaws that the construction and use of these tables.[470] Because of these reasons this practice has received particular attention in the literature. Building on this strand of research, in the following I will focus exclusively on targeting that may derive from the employment of statistical tables.

---

467 Sugarman Stephen, 1985. Doing Away with Tort Law. 73(3) CAL. L. REV. 555.

468 Dewees Don and Michael Trebilcock, 1992. The Efficacy of the Tort System and Its Alternatives: A Review of Empirical Evidence. 30 OSGOODE HALL L. J., 57; Dewees Donald et al., 1996. Exploring the Domain of Accident Law: Taking the Facts Seriously. Oxford University Press on Demand; Ben van Velthoven, 2009. Empirics of Tort, In Tort Law and Economics, Ed. Michael Faure, 2nd Edition, EDWARD ELGAR, 453.

469 Wriggins (2007). Chamallas and Wriggins (2010).

470 Avraham and Yuracko (2017).

5.4 Gender and Race-Based Statistical Tables: A Comparative Analysis

Having explained the dynamics that lead to targeting, the next section discusses the employment of gender and race based statistical tables in various jurisdictions. Since a large part of the literature on the employment of group-specific statistical tables comes from the US, the starting point of this analysis is the US tort law practice. The analysis is then extended to three European countries: England, France and Italy. The purpose of this section is to understand whether issues arising from the employment of these tables in US trials are present also in European tort law. I focus on England, France and Italy in order to account for potential discrepancies that may arise from differences in the legal traditions (Common law-Civil law) within the European experience. Among the European countries that adopt a Civil-law system, I chose to compare Italy and France because in a legal analysis that is built along gender and racial issues, it can be interesting to compare countries in which different situations prevail in this respect. In this regard, France has experienced strong immigration from African countries starting from the 1950's;[471] while in Italy the phenomenon is much more recent.[472] Similarly, women's job market conditions (which are reflected in statistical tables) are quite different in these two countries. With women scoring relatively better in terms of employment rate in France than in Italy and a much lower gender pay gap in Italy than in France.[473] Thus, the rate at which courts have been confronted with racial/gender issues related to socioeconomic measures reflected in statistical tables might be very different in the two countries.

5.4.1 Gender and Race-Based Statistical Tables in the US

As recently highlighted by Avraham and Yuracko,[474] gender and race have a major role in determining damages under US tort law. This role is largely due to the employment of gender and race-based statistical tables. In this section, I discuss

---

471 Vladescu, Eloisa, 2006. The Assimilation of Immigrant Groups in France–Myth or Reality?. 5(39) JEAN MONNET/ROBERT SCHUMAN PAPER SERIES, 1.

472 European Commission, 2006. European Migration Network Impact of Immigration on Europe's Societies.

473 See:http://ec.europa.eu/eurostat/statistics-explained/index.php/Gender_statistics

474 Avraham and Yurako (2017).

US courts' use of these tables as a basis for the comparative analysis that will follow.

A victim's life expectancy is a major component for the establishment of two types of damages:[475] i) future expenses that the victim will have to bear because of the tort (e.g. medical bills); ii) damages for future pain and suffering. In this connection, under US tort law life expectancy is usually determined based on the life expectancy tables provided by the US Federal Government.[476] These tables differentiate life expectancy depending on gender and (certain) racial/ethnic groups. In this regard, note that, in the US, females have on average a higher life expectancy than males (respectively about 81 and 76 years) and Black people a significantly lower one than White people.[477] Without distinguishing by gender, Black people have a life expectancy of 75 years compared with the 79 years of White people.[478]

Starting from the values contained in these tables, forensic economists called to provide expert testimony in court adjust these life values based on the particular circumstances of the case.[479] For instance, if some aspect of the (pre-accident) health condition of the victim suggests that her life expectancy is lower than average, the abovementioned value will be adjusted accordingly. In performing these adjustments expert testimony rely often on statistics (e.g. relative mortality ratios which take into account, for instance, a particular medical condition or whether the victim is a smoker) that are further divided along gender and racial lines.[480] This may provide additional room for gender and racial discrepancies in the determination of damages at trial.[481] Lastly, the estimations based on these data can be

---

475 Ibid.

476 Richard Singer, 2005. How to Prepare a Life Expectancy Report for an Attorney in a Tort Case, 37 J. INS. MED. 42.

477 See U.S. DEP'T OF HEALTH AND HUM. SERV, HEALTH, UNITED STATES, WITH SPECIAL FEATURE ON RACIAL AND ETHNIC HEALTH DISPARITIES, table 15 (2015) https://www.cdc.gov/nchs/data/hus/hus15.pdf. It is important to stress that not all racial minorities score worse than Whites when it comes to life expectancy. Noticeably, Asians' longevity is significantly higher than that of any other racial group (86 years in 2009). See THE HENRY J. KAISER FAMILY FOUNDATION, 2009. LIFE EXPECTANCY AT BIRTH (IN YEARS), BY RACE/ETHNICITY, http://kff.org/other/state-indicator/life-expectancy-by-re/?currentTimeframe=0.

478 U.S. DEP'T OF HEALTH AND HUM. SERV. (2015).

479 Avraham and Yuracko (2017).

480 Ibid.

481 Ibid.

further adjusted by jurors, which are called to adapt them to the specific situation of the victim.[482]

Similarly, the estimation of the losses for future earning capacity are highly influenced by the employment of work-life expectancy tables.[483] These tables provide courts with information regarding the time period for which the victim was expected to earn a (higher) wage had the accident not occurred. Also these tables are often divided by gender and race. Based on these tables the computation of the losses for future earning capacity is obtained by multiplying the expected future yearly wages by the expected number of working years. This time period is shorter for females than for males and for Black people than for White people.[484] The resulting sum is then sometimes adjusted by juries on the basis of the particular circumstances of the case.[485]

Lastly, in situations in which the past earnings of the victim are not available (e.g., because she is too young to have a job) or when there are reasons to believe that her future earnings would have been different from the past ones, damages are sometimes based on the average national wage.[486] Data on the average national wage is taken from the dataset provided by the Bureau of Labor Statistics, which differentiates average wages across gender and racial groups.[487] As discussed above, these values are higher for males than for females and for Whites than for Blacks. The estimations resulting from this calculus are subsequently adapted based on the specific circumstances of the case.

Along with these general trends, a few courts have recently moved towards the use of blended tables.[488] For instance, in *Wheeler* and *Tarpeh-Doe* the court adopted a race-neutral approach to establish damages for a mixed-race tort victim. Similarly, in *US v. Bedonie*,[489] the district court has ruled that the use of gender and race-based damages estimations may sometimes not be warranted and that it is for the alleged tortfeasor to prove that differentiated damages awards are justified in the specific case at hand. This approach has been subsequently endorsed

482 Ibid.

483 Ibid.

484 Ibid.

485 Ibid.

486 Ibid.

487 Ibid.

488 Ibid.

489 United States v. Bedonie, 317 F. Supp. 2d 1285, 1319 (D. Utah 2004).

by the Tenth Circuit, which, however, has also specified that it is in the discretion of the lower court whether to apply differentiated estimations based on gender and race.[490] Note that in *US v. Bedonie*, the reasoning of the court was largely based on the observation that the use of gender/race based tables was ethically unwarranted as it would have led to discriminative outcomes and to the perpetuation of existing stereotypes.[491] In a few other cases, the practice of using differentiated tables has been abandoned on a (partially) different ground, namely on the idea that gender and racial disparities captured by these tables are unlikely to accurately capture future socioeconomic trends.[492]

In conclusion, as recently highlighted by Avraham and Yuracko, the use of gender/race blended tables to establish tort damages is more an exception than the rule in current US tort law.[493] In the next section, I analyze whether similar trends are observable in the Italian experience.

5.4.2 Gender and Race-Based Statistical Tables in Italy

The use of statistical tables to determine damages in tort trials is not foreign to the Italian experience. Yet, the relevance of race and gender for the establishment of damages is much more limited than under US law. Firstly, with some exception,[494] Italian authorities do not collect data on life expectancy, work-life expectancy, and average wage according to race or ethnicity. Maybe also due to this circumstance, under Italian law, the only relevant distinction in the employment of statistical tables in tort trials is gender.

Generally, the compensation of losses for future earning capacity can take two main forms: a lump sum or a rent. When the lump sum approach is adopted, Italian courts have often relied on the following computational method: multiplying the decrease in the yearly net wage due to the accident by a capitalization rate.[495] Until recently, Italian courts have adopted capitalization rates set by the

---

490 United States v. Serawop, 505 F.3d 1112, at 1126 (10th Cir. 2007).

491 Bedonie, 317 F. Supp. 2d at 1319.

492 Reilly v. United States, 665 F. Supp. 976, 997 (D.R.I. 1987).

493 Avraham and Yuracko (2017).

494 See, e.g., Ministero della Salute, 2016. Piano d'Azione Salute per e con le Comunità Rom, Sinti e Caminanti, http://www.salute.gov.it/imgs/C_17_pubblicazioni_2451_allegato.pdf.

495 This capitalization rate already takes into account the discount rate to be applied for the time difference between when the lump sum is received and the time in which these wages would have been earned had the victim not been involved in the accident. See Enzo Ronchi et al., 2015.

Royal Decree (R.D.) 9 October 1922, n. 1403.[496] These rates were calculated based on the mortality tables gaged from the 1911 census of the Italian population. Thus, the capitalization rate was based on a life expectancy of 54.9 years, which was the expected life of an average Italian (not considering gender disparities) in 1911. Italian courts have long adopted various strategies to reconcile the discrepancy between life expectancy and work-life expectancy. For instance, to account for this difference, courts were expected to decrease the amount resulting from the above mentioned calculus by 20/30%.[497] However, courts have often avoided utilizing this reduction to make up for the life expectancy changes since 1911. Indeed, life expectancy today in Italy is considerably higher than in 1911, with males averaging 80 years and about 85 years for females.[498] Because the capitalization rate adopted by R.D. n. 1403 did not distinguish between genders, the resulting amounts were equal for men and women.

The discrepancy between men and women's life expectancy was addressed in 2015 when the Corte di Cassazione (the Italian Supreme Court) adopted a new approach directing lower courts to use more recent life expectancy tables that provide different values for gender.[499] This decision was adopted on various grounds, two of which were: i) to provide a more accurate estimate of the losses suffered by victims; and ii) to provide different estimates for males and females. The Court did not impose a specific source to be used for the determination of these losses, yet it indicated as a possible source the criteria listed in the Quaderni del CSM, 1990, n. 41 (hereinafter "CSM41").[500] The CSM41 contains updated capitalization rates that discern based on gender.[501]

Guida alla valutazione medico-legale dell'invalidità permanente 69 (2d ed.). For a full discussion of the methods used to calculate damages related to losses of future earning capacity, see id. at 60-80.

496 § 77.4.2 - R.D. 9 ottobre 1922, n. 1403. Approvazione delle nuove tariffe per la costituzione delle rendite vitalizie della Cassa nazionale per le assicurazioni sociali, available at: http://www.edizionieuropee.it/LAW/HTML/40/zn77_04_002.html.

497 Ronchi et al. (2015).

498 Popolazione e Famiglie, Italian National Institute. NAT'L INST. OF STAT., http://www.istat.it/it/anziani/popolazione-e-famiglie (last visited Feb. 19, 2018).

499 Cass sez. ter., 14 ottobre 2015, n. 20615.

500 Ibid.

501 Consiglio Superiore della Magistratura, 1990. Nuovi Orientamenti e Nuovi Criteri Per la Determinazione del Danno, QUADERNI DEL. CSM, N. 41 (1990), http://www.csm.it/web/csm-internet/norme-e-documenti/dettaglio/-/asset_publisher/YoFfLzL3vKc1/content/quaderno-n-41-1990 [hereinafter CSM41].

Following the suggestion by the Supreme Court, lower courts have started abandoning the use of the tables contained in the R.D. n. 1403 in favor of the new approach. For instance, in a recent medical malpractice case, the Tribunale di Como (the Court of Como) issued a decision on the losses of future earning capacity on the basis of the criteria contained in the CSM41.[502] The court estimated that the accident reduced the ability of the victim to earn by 15%. The computation for the estimation of the losses was therefore the following: annual earnings (net of taxes) multiplied by the gender-based capitalization coefficient (CSM41), with the product multiplied by 15%. Subsequently, a similar calculation was applied by the Tribunale di Parma (the Court of Parma) in a traffic accident case.[503] There, however, the Court of Parma decided to reduce the damages award by 20% to account for the difference between life expectancy and work-life expectancy. The court did not refer to whether a different reduction would apply had the victim been of a different gender. Thus, despite in Italy work-life expectancy is higher for males than for females, this factor is not taken into account when determining damages awards.[504]

Differences by gender are also not particularly relevant in the determination of the wage applicable for the abovementioned calculation. In fact, courts usually rely on various measures of income (decreased by the residual earning capacity) that do not differentiate by gender. One example of this is the national average wage or the average wage for the particular industry in which the victim was expected to work in the future.[505] When the victim is a child and/or it is difficult to forecast the future employment of the victim, courts rely on measures of income adjusted on the basis of the socioeconomic status of the family of the victim, but no distinction is made for gender.[506]

Similarly, under current Italian practice, the use of gender-based statistical tables has only a residual role concerning the award of non-economic losses. In actuality, these losses are determined using computational methods that take into

---

502 Trib. del Como, 14 gennaio 2016, n. 27.

503 Trib. del Parma, 25 maggio 2016, n. 726.

504 However, the higher work-life expectancy of males (forty-five years) compared to females (forty years) in Italy is recognized in the assessment of the social costs of car accidents performed by the Italian government. See e.g., Ministero delle Infrastrutture e dei Trasporti, 2014. Studio di valutazione dei Costi Sociali dell'Incidentalità Stradale, dell'incidentalità stradale 7, http://www.mit.gov.it/mit/mop_all.php?p_id=12919.

505 Ronchi et al. 2015.

506 Ibid.

account the age of the victim, but generally does not differentiate across gender groups. This occurs, for instance, with regards to the "danno biologico," which is awarded to victims who have suffered a decrease in their enjoyment of life as a result of the tort. This type of damages is a major component of pain and suffering damages compensated under Italian law.[507] The "danno biologico" is determined from a strict calculation based on tables prepared by committees of lawyers, judges and actuaries at the court level. Among the various tables elaborated by lower courts, the Italian Supreme Court has indicated use the tables set forth by the Tribunal of Milan as the preferable one.[508] These tables provide invalidity points ranging from 1% to 100% (with 100% representing permanent complete invalidity), to which corresponds a pecuniary value depending on the age of the victim (regardless of gender).

In this context, the residual role played by gender is relegated to situations in which the circumstances of the case are peculiar to an extent that judges prefer to award damages partially departing from the abovementioned method. For instance, in a recent case, the Tribunale di Padova (Court of Padova) found that the application of the Milano tables would have led to a too low damages award.[509] This decision was motivated on two grounds: (1) the victim at the time of the accident had an expected life of about 50 years (given that she was 35 and life expectancy for women in Italy is about 85 years); and (2) the significant negative impact that the accident had on the life of the victim. From the decision, the temporal factor (i.e. the life expectancy of the victim), seems to have influenced the decision of the court. In this connection, it is not clear whether the court would have reached the same conclusion had the victim been a male (whose residual life expectancy would have therefore been around 45 years and thus shorter than the one of the victim of the accident). In this case, the court explicitly mentioned that the substantial residual life expectancy of the victim was a relevant criterion to justify the application of a different calculation than the one usually adopted, but did not specify the year threshold after which such treatment would have been justified. In this sense, gender-based life expectancy tables may sometimes impact court decisions on damages for non-pecuniary losses. Yet, their impact is (at best) relegated to exceptional circumstances.

---

507 Ibid.

508 See, e.g., Cass., sez. ter., 15 ottobre 2015, n. 20895.

509 Tribunale del Padova, 20 maggio 2016, n. 1579.

Lastly, gender-based statistical tables on life expectancy are sometimes used to establish future expenses due to the accident. Here, the higher life expectancy of females often translates into higher damages awards.

5.4.3 Gender and Race-Based Statistical Tables in England

As under Italian law, English courts do not make use of race-based statistical tables to award damages. Thus, in the following I will focus solely on the gender side of the issue.

In the English practice, damages awards for future losses of income capacity and future expenses are usually awarded in the form of lump-sums.[510] Generally, the estimation of losses of future earnings is carried out on the basis of the Ogden Tables.[511] The Working Party, consisting of actuaries, lawyers, accountants, and other interested parties, produces and regularly updates these tables. The Ogden Tables provide a detailed set of procedures to be followed in the estimation of lump sum damages for losses of earning capacity and future expenses.[512] The basic procedure suggested by the Working Party consists in multiplying the annual expected loss/expense by a multiplier which gives the present capital value of the loss/expense.[513] Multipliers differ depending on whether the loss is expected to: (1) continue for the whole life of the victim; (2) continue until the retirement of the victim; or (3) start from the retirement of the victim.[514] Given the higher life expectancy of females, multipliers are higher for females than for males. The estimated sum is then adjusted for factors other than mortality (i.e. education, disa-

---

510 Cees van Dam, 2013. European Tort Law, OXFORD UNIVERSITY PRESS, 361 (2d ed.).

511 U.K. GOV. ACTUARY DEP'T, ACTUARIAL TABLES WITH EXPLANATORY NOTES FOR USE IN PERSONAL INJURY AND FATAL ACCIDENT CASES (7th ed. 2011), https://www.gov.uk/government/uploads/system/uploads/attachment_data/file/245859/ogden_tables_7th_edition.pdf (hereinafter OGDEN TABLES). For courts' use of these tables see, e.g., Royal Victoria Infirmary and Associated Hospitals NHS Trust v. B (Child) [2002] EWCA Civ 348 (QB); Woodward v. Leeds Teaching Hospitals NHS Trust [2012] EWHC 2167. (QB).

512 OGDEN TABLES (2011).

513 Ibid.

514 Ibid.

bility and employment status). This is done by multiplying the previously established sum by a number tailored to these factors.[515] Here, the multipliers are generally higher for men because of their longer work-life expectancy.[516] The resulting sum is then adjusted on the basis of the specific circumstances of the case.[517]

Gender plays a role also in establishing the wage that the victim was expected to have earned had the accident not occurred. This issue was discussed in length in *Van Wees v. Karkour*, in which the judge established that the gender wage gap reported in official statistical tables should be reflected in damages awards.[518] However, the court also argued that these tables capture only a snapshot of reality and that the wage gap will decrease in the future.[519] This factor must also be taken into account when awarding damages.[520] In addition, when the victim is a child and thus the circumstances of the case leave high uncertainty regarding her loss of earning capacity, the awards are tailored on the socioeconomic status of the parents of the victim.[521] Here, no difference is made on the basis of gender.

Just like in Italian law, the estimation of non-economic losses is mainly carried out without making reference to the pre-accident life expectancy of the victim.[522] In fact, courts usually determine pain and suffering damages on the basis of the "Guidelines for the Assessment of General Damages in Personal Injury Cases."[523] The guidelines are not binding, but in the absence of particular reasons that suggest adopting a different computational method, courts tend to follow them

515 Ibid.

516 Ibid.

517 Ibid.

518 Van Wees v. Karkour [2007] EWHC (QB),165, 165 (Eng.). (Gender-based tables were also accepted as a legitimate source of information in the more recent case: Kate Emma Woodward v. Leeds Teaching Hospitals NHS Trust Case [2012] EWHC 2167. However, here, the judge decided not to rely on these numbers because these tables (which focused only on one industry) were not applicable to the case).

519 Van Wees v. Karkour [2007] EWHC (QB) 165. (Eng.).

520 Ibid.

521 Ken Oliphant, 2006. Children as Victims under the Law of England and Wales, in Children in Tort Law Part II: Children as Victims, 82, (Martín-Casals ed.), SPRINGER-VERLAG/WIEN.

522 William Rogers, 2006. England – Non-Pecuniary Loss Under English Law, in Damages for Non-Pecuniary Loss in a Comparative, 61 (William V.H. Rogers ed.), SPRINGER.

523 Ken Oliphant, 2008. England and Wales, in European Tort Law, 213 (Koziol & Steininger ed.), SPRINGER. For the guidelines see: McKay, Colin and Great Britain Judicial Studies Board, 2010. Guidelines for the Assessment of General Damages in Personal Injury Cases (OXFORD UNIVERSITY PRESS).

in assessing pain and suffering awards.[524] The guidelines contain ranges of awards per type of injury that are based on the amount of damages awarded in previous cases. It is worth noting that the damages awards for pain and suffering contained in these tables are often calibrated on the basis of the age and the life expectancy of the victim.[525] Yet, the Guidelines do not provide different ranges of awards based on gender. Thus, in general, the higher life expectancy of a female may be reflected in the damages awards in a particular case, but this higher award may be reflected in subsequent cases regardless of whether the victim is a male or a female.

5.4.4 Gender and Race Based Statistical Tables in France

Similar to the Italian and the English experience, the racial group of the victim has no bearing in the determination of losses in French tort trials. Yet, gender influences the determination of the losses via the use of statistical tables. The life expectancy of the victim influences damages awards for future losses of income capacity and future expenses. Lump-sums are the common way in which these types of damages are awarded in French law.[526] The determination of these type of damages is obtained by multiplying the expected loss of income (or the expense) by a capitalization rate indicated in the tables published on the Gazette du Palais on April 26th, 2016 (n° 16).[527] These capitalization rates are based on the life expectancy of the French population in the period 2006-2008 and take into account an inflation rate of 1.04%.[528] The tables provide different rates depending on the period for which the victim is expected to suffer the loss. For instance, depending on whether the victim was expected to receive her last wage at 62 or 68 years old, the rate applicable for the calculation varies (ceteris paribus it is higher at 68 than at 62).[529] The tables distinguish between male and female with the latter having a

524 Oliphant (2008).

525 Avraham and Yuracko (2017).

526 Benoît Mornet, 2015. L'Indemnisation des Préjudices en Cas de Blessures ou de Décès, 1, 27, available at https://www.avocats-toulouse.com/wp-content/uploads/2015/10/Referentiel-Mornet-2015.pdf.

527 Capitalization Schedule 2016 of the Gazette du Palais (n° 16), ACTUALITÉS (Apr. 26, 2016), available at http://www.gazettedupalais.com/services/actualites/vie_pro/e-docs/bareme_de_-capitalisation_2016_de_la_gazette_du_palais/document_actu_pro.phtml?cle_doc=00002E02.

528 Ibid.

529 Ibid.

higher rate reflecting their longer life expectancy. Contrary to English law, the resulting sum is not adjusted on the basis of factors other than mortality. In addition, the loss is not adjusted on the basis of gender differences in work-life expectancy. As a consequence, and everything else equal, the sum remains higher for females than for males.

Just like under Italian law, gender-based wage differences, while existent,[530] are not reflected in damages awards. Instead, courts adopt either the French minimum wage (SMIC), the national average wage, or the average wage of the industry where the victim was (expected) to be employed.[531] No differentiation is made on the basis of gender. With regards to children or other situations in which it is difficult to estimate what would have been the average wage of the victim, damages are adjusted on the basis of factors such as a woman's educational level and the socioeconomic status of her family.[532]

As to the estimation of non-economic losses, differences in life expectancy are generally not reflected in damages awards. Among the various types of non-economic losses compensated under French law,[533] the age of the victim is considered only for the establishment of the "déficit fonctionnel permanent."[534] The quantification of this type of damage is made following a two-step procedure. First, a sum determined on the basis of the age of the victim and the degree of invalidity caused by the accident (this invalidity is expressed as a percentage, with 100% being full invalidity).[535] The tables that provide the resulting sums vary depending on the Court of Appeal (Court d'Appel) considered. Second, this sum is then multiplied by the invalidity point (not expressed as a percentage) to obtain the full amount of damages.[536] For instance, following the tables established by

530 See, for instance, the recent estimates made by the French National Institute of Statistics and Economic Studies: Thomas Morin and Nathan Remila, Le Revenu Salarial des Femmes Reste Inférieur à Celui des Hommes, INSEE, N° 1436. (2013), available at https://www.insee.fr/fr/statistiques/1280986.

531 Bernard Dubuisson, 2013. Le Dommage et sa Reparation, par. 27, Larcier. For an application of the calculus see, for instance, Cour de Cassation, 19 février 2014, n° 13-11360.

532 See Mornet (2015).

533 Michel Cannarsa, 2002. Compensation for Personal Injury in France, 1, available at http://www.jus.unitn.it/cardozo/review/2002/cannarsa.pdf; Benoît Mornet, 2015. L'Indemnisation des Préjudices en Cas de Blessures ou de Décès, 1, 27, available at https://www.avocats-toulouse.com/wp-content/uploads/2015/10/Referentiel-Mornet-2015.pdf.

534 See Mornet (2015).

535 Ibid.

536 Ibid.

the Court of Appeal of Toulouse in 2010,[537] an invalidity point of 50% suffered by a victim of age 20, corresponds to a sum of €2810 Euros, which is then multiplied by 50 resulting in a damage award of €140,500 Euros.[538] Gender plays no role in this estimation.[539]

5.4.5 Comparative Analysis on Targeting Incentives

In the previous section, I have discussed the employment of gender and race-based statistical tables for the determination of damages under US, English, French and Italian tort law. When read in conjunction with the discussion of the relation between the use of gender/race based tables and targeting,[540] the analysis provides a comparative assessment of whether, and to what extent, courts' practice incentivizes to tortfeasors to target a specific social group identified either by gender or race.

With regards to race, the analysis has shown that under English, French and Italian law courts do not use race-based statistical tables to determine the relevant measures of socioeconomic status. Thus, contrary to the US experience, targeting based on the use of statistical tables is unlikely to take place in these three jurisdictions.

Conversely, the analysis has highlighted that gender does play a role in the determination of damages across all the jurisdictions considered. Yet, the effect of gender is different in the three legal systems. We have seen that the employment of gender-based wage tables takes place both under US and English law. However, in the latter, courts tend to adjust the calculations based on these tables on the basis of the job market improvements that women are likely to experience in the coming future. This, in turn mitigates the targeting incentives provided by the gender wage gap captured by current statistics. The French and the Italian practice are instead insensitive to gender wage gaps, and therefore no incentives for targeting do exist in these jurisdictions with regards to this component of damages.

537 Cours D'Appel de Agen, Angers, Bordeaux, Grenoble, Limoges, Nîmes, Orleans, Pau, Potiers, Toulouse, Référentiel Indiatif Régional de L'Indemnisation Du Dommage Corporel, 1, 12, (Nov. 2010), available at https://www.avocats-toulouse.com/IMG/pdf/RIRIDC-NOV.2010.pdf.

538 Mornet (2015)

539 Ibid.

540 See Avraham and Yuracko (2017).

Similarly, France seems to be the most pro-female jurisdiction, followed by Italy, when it comes to the employment of life and work-life expectancy tables. In this regard, the current practices followed by Italian and French courts take into account gender gaps only with regards to life expectancy, which is the only measure on which females score better than males. In this sense, the use of statistical tables in Italy may provide a marginal targeting incentive to the tortfeasor to the disadvantage of males. In Italy, this incentive is likely to be small especially because pain and suffering awards are generally not established on the basis of life expectancy tables. Thus, the incentive exists solely with regards to future expenses (e.g. medical bills). In French practice, the incentive might be more substantial (yet, still limited) as the life expectancy of the victim also affects the determination of loss of future income capacity.

Conversely, both English and US law take into account gender gaps in life expectancy and work-life expectancy. Since gender gaps in these two measures go in different directions, whether a victim will receive higher compensation being a male or a female depends on the specific circumstances of the case. It is beyond the scope of the present article to establish whether, overall, this practice provides incentives for targeting one of the two groups. However, notice that the fact that life expectancy plays less of a role in determining pain and suffering awards under English law limits the potential benefits that females derive from the use of gender-based tables in tort trials.

Table 2 Use of Non-Blended Tables for Damages Awards

	Race				Gender		
	Average Wage	Life Expect-ancy	Work-Life Expectancy		Average Wage	Life Expectancy	Work-Life Expectancy
England	No	No	No		Yes	Yes	Yes
France	No	No	No		No	Yes	No
Italy	No	No	No		No	Yes	No
US	Yes	Yes	Yes		Yes	Yes	Yes

5.5 The Neoclassical Law and Economics of Targeting

When viewed through the lenses of law and economics, the primary aim of tort law is to provide incentives to tortfeasors and victims to take optimal precautions and engage in their activity at an optimal level.[541] Given this goal, conventional law and economics may support the use of non-blended tables. This view has been recently questioned.[542] This section will review these two opposing views on the subject matter.

5.5.1 The Law and Economics Arguments Pro Non-Blended Tables

Classical law and economics provide two prima facie arguments in favor of the use of non-blended tables, one relates to victim's willingness to pay (WTP) for reductions in expected losses, and the second is concerned with the use of income as a proxy for productivity. In the latter argument, economists and economically minded legal scholars tend to see income as a proxy for productivity, which is often considered a social value.[543] In this view, to the extent that female and minority members earn less and work for a shorter period than white males, targeting will reduce not only the private costs but also the social costs of the activity of the tortfeasor.[544]

Looking at the same issue from another perspective, targeting receives support from the law and economics because if blended tables were adopted, tort law could provide distorted price signals to tortfeasors regarding the amount to be invested in precautionary measures.[545] This would occur if the optimal amount of precautions that a tortfeasor should take was determined on the basis of how much a victim would be willing to pay to avoid being exposed to the risk of suffering the loss. Notice that in law and economics this is a very common way of determining the optimal investments of tortfeasors, as it is often held that investments in precautions should be tailored to reductions in expected losses.[546]

---

541 Guido Calabresi, 1970. The Cost of Accidents: A Legal and Economic Analysis, YALE UNIVERSITY PRESS (New Haven).

542 Avraham and Yuracko (2017).

543 Ibid.

544 Ibid.

545 Ibid.

546 Porat (2011).

If the WTP of a victim is accepted as the preferable way of establishing care investments of tortfeasors, the use of blended tables may provide distorted incentives by decreasing tortfeasors' ability to discern between differences in WTP of different victims.[547] In fact, the WTP to avoid injuries or death is generally positively correlated with the wealth of the individual. This is due to the strict constraints that relatively less wealthy people have in terms of their spending capacity and, maybe, to the expected higher losses in future earning capacity that high-income earners face.[548] When damage awards do not distinguish between the WTP of the victims, tortfeasors will be incentivized to invest to an excessive (too little) extent in precautionary measures to avoid harming the less (more) wealthy.[549] One could argue that this argument does not apply here because statistical tables capture income instead of wealth gaps. However, while the WTP of victims is more related to their wealth than to their income,[550] since income and wealth are often strongly correlated, the argument is still relevant. Notice also that this issue is not solved completely by the use of gender/race-based statistical tables, as relying on them can at best make the determination of damages closer to the average of each group considered. Thus, to the extent that groups are not completely homogeneous and tortfeasors are not able to target victims if not on the basis of group, some over/under-investment will take place. Based on these arguments, conventional law and economics indeed favor targeting.[551]

Avraham and Yorako have recently proposed several arguments on the basis of which targeting may not be efficient.[552] The next section will briefly review these arguments which represent the basis of the behavioral analysis that follows.

5.5.2 Neoclassical Arguments Against Non-Blended Tables

A recent article by Avraham and Yuracko, has put forward a powerful critique of the conventional law and economics view regarding the use of non-blended tables.553 This critique is built upon four main arguments that will be reviewed.

---

547 Avraham and Yuracko (2017).

548 Ibid.

549 Ibid.

550 Porat (2011).

551 Avraham and Yuracko (2017).

552 Ibid.

553 Ibid.

The first argument proposed by Avraham and Yuracko relates to the inaccuracy of non-blended tables. Due to this inaccuracy, the use of non-blended tables might result in less accurate determination of damages than the use of blended ones.[554] This argument is based on two main observations. First, tables of this type can in fact only capture a snapshot of reality, and are thus unable to take into account the dynamic aspects of gender and racial groups socioeconomic status.[555] In particular, they do not consider trends showing improvements in the socioeconomic conditions of females and racial minorities that have taken place in the recent past.[556] For instance, these tables do not capture the advancements that, thanks to better educational achievements, young women have achieved in the labor market of several US metropolitan cities.[557] The inability of these tables to capture dynamic trends, is manifest in their imprecision in forecasting future dynamics of racial group measures of socioeconomic status.558 For instance, according to the projections released in 1995 by the Census Bureau, the life expectancy at birth of a Black male in 2015 was expected to be 62.5 years.[559] If we look at the actual life expectancy at birth of a Black man in 2014 it was 72.5.[560] Thus projections made about 20 years ago underestimated the 2015 life expectancy of Black males by 10 years. Conversely, for White males the underestimation was only 4 years,561 indicating that these tables failed to capture the improvements that Black males would have achieved in the period considered. Notice that forecasted measures are based on past trends.[562] Thus, given the observed discrepancy between forecasted at actual values, this indicates that these tables are not particularly accurate in cap-

554 Ibid.

555 Ibid.

556 Ibid.

557 Ibid.

558 For a method to forecast the socioeconomic status of racial groups, see Dominioni et al. (2018).

559 See US Bureau of the Census, Current Population Reports, Population Projections of the United States by Age, Sex, Race, and Hispanic Origin: 1995 to 2050, 2 (1995), https://www.census.gov/prod/1/pop/p25-1130/p251130.pdf.

560 US Department of Health and Human Services, Health, United States, 2015, With Special Feature on Racial and Ethnic Health Disparities, Table 15, 53 (2015), https://www.cdc.gov/nchs/data/hus/hus15.pdf.

561 Compare US Bureau of the Census, supra note 112 with US Department of Health and Human Services, Health, United States, 2015, With Special Feature on Racial and Ethnic Health Disparities, Table 15, (2015), https://www.cdc.gov/nchs/data/hus/hus15.pdf.

562 US Bureau of the Census, supra note 112.

turing dynamic trends. Notice also that similar issues arise when focusing on gender gaps. For instance, statistical tables report that females tend to earn considerably less than males of the same age. However, several studies have shown that the gender income gap is narrowing in many industries as females are improving their job market positioning.[563]

The overall conclusion is that non-blended tables are likely to lead to systematic underestimations of the damages awarded to females and minority members. In this regard, as mentioned above, the economics of tort law highlights that systematic underestimations of damages awarded can lead tortfeasors to underinvest in precautionary measures and engage too much in the potentially tortious activity to the detriment of social welfare.564

Second, according to Avraham and Yuracko, the inherently lower accuracy of non-blended tables could be linked to the way these tables are built and used. In particular, they notice that by reporting means, these tables fail to account for the (often high) variability of these measures.[565] In this connection, a clear example of a minority population that is often treated as a single group but that has a strong variability in terms of the socioeconomic status of its members are Asians in the US population. This "homogeneous" racial group is in fact composed of different sub-ethnic groups, some of which score better than Whites on several dimensions of socioeconomic status, while others are in more precarious conditions than the average Black person.566 Avraham and Yuracko argue that using blended tables may decrease the variance in damages awarded as they are built upon a larger number of observations than non-blended ones.[567] This, in turn, can be social welfare enhancing, when it leads to a large number of victims to be miscompensated by a little, than when it leads to a smaller amount of larger misconceptions.568 This is because risk averse individuals, i.e. individuals that do not like having to

563 See, for instance, Laura Cox Kaplan, How Young Women Are Changing the Workplace, WORLD ECONOMIC FORUM, (Oct. 29, 2014), https://www.weforum.org/agenda/2014/10/millennial-women-changing-workplace/; see also Cate Doty, Addressing the Gender Gap in College Aspirations, N.Y. TIMES (Oct. 23, 2009), https://thechoice.blogs.nytimes.com/2009/10/23/addressing-the-gender-gap-in-colleges/; see also Avraham and Yuracko (2017).

564 See supra Introduction; see also Avraham and Yuracko (2017).

565 See Avraham and Yuracko (2017).

566 Arthur Sakamoto, et al. 2009. Socioeconomic Attainments of Asian Americans, 35 ANNUAL REVIEW OF SOCIOLOGY 255.

567 Avraham and Yuracko (2017).

568 Avraham and Yuracko 2017.

bear a pure financial risk,569 often prefer suffering a smaller loss than having a small chance to suffer a large one.570 Yet, whether increasing the number of observations necessarily leads to lower the variance in damages awarded is however not mathematically guaranteed.571 As such, the argument is not very powerful.

Similarly, the use of means, which are particularly sensitive to outliers, may fail to capture skewed distributions in measures of socioeconomic status across racial and gender groups. This, according to Avraham and Yuracko, can be problematic because if the distribution of the socioeconomic measure considered is positively skewed for the relatively better-positioned group and the opposite is true for the disadvantaged group, it can be that statistically significant differences between the means of the two distributions are not mirrored in statistically significant differences between modes and medians.[572] This suggests that the use of means might be less justified than previously thought. This is particularly true in the context of tort law, where the courts apply a more likely than not standard to reduce errors in adjudication.[573] They therefore, suggest using modes or medians as alternative measures. [574] In a nutshell, Avraham and Yuracko's first argument is that the use of non-blended tables may lead to unwarranted targeting, i.e. to targeting that is not justified on the basis of the actual social costs of the activity of the tortfeasor.[575]

A second argument put forward by Avraham and Yuracko relates to the dynamics that lead to gaps in socioeconomic status between the considered groups.[576] In particular, they argue that the lower socioeconomic standing of minorities and women in society is a result of market failures.[577] For instance, they highlight that employers perceive lower job attachment by female and minority members, and thus offer jobs that take less into account the needs of these segments of the population.[578] As a consequence, job attachment of women and minority members may be further eroded. To the extent that employers' perceptions do not reflect

569 On risk aversion see Shavell (2004).

570 See Avraham and Yuracko 2017.

571 Ibid.

572 Ibid.

573 Ibid.

574 Ibid.

575 Ibid.

576 Ibid.

577 Ibid.

578 Ibid.

innate preferences of females (which may on average have a stronger preference to be directly involved in child raising) and minority members, this labor discrimination is inefficient.[579] The result of this vicious circle, when mirrored in damages awards may provide an ex-ante incentive to members of minority groups and females to reduce investments in human capital. This, according to Avraham and Yuracko could be inefficient, as it may lead a potentially productive member of society to underinvest in productive skills.[580] However, while these incentives might well be present, they are unlikely to be particularly strong. Indeed, as Avraham and Yuracko themselves recognize, it is hard to believe that the use of non-blended tables may induce members of discriminated groups or their agents (e.g. parents towards children) to underinvest in productive skills.[581] The argument, while logically strong, remains weak.[582]

Third, in Avraham and Yuracko's view, it is ethically inappropriate to consider the WTP of victims to reduce the expected losses from accidents.[583] Recently, law and economics scholars have put forward various arguments against the use of WTP to establish amounts that victims are willing to invest to reduce expected losses.[584] As noted above, the WTP of a person is largely determined by her wealth. In this connection, the wealthy person's WTP will be higher than the one of a less wealthy person, partially because the former has a greater possibility to spend her (greater) wealth in activities from which she derives utility. Porat and Tabbach have recently shown that efficiency does not require considering the increase in WTP linked to the desire to spend wealth when setting damages.[585] This is because wealth is an inherently transferable good and the law should not be concerned with who enjoys it, but only about its production.[586] Avraham and Yuracko go further than this. In their perspective, for ethical reasons differences in human capital, linked to belonging to a certain racial or gender group, should not be taken into account when establishing damages awards.[587]

---

579 Ibid.

580 Ibid.

581 Ibid.

582 Ibid.

583 Ibid.

584 Ariel Porat and Avraham Tabbach, 2011. Willingness to Pay, Death, Wealth, and Damages, 13 AM. L. & ECON. REV. 45.

585 Ibid.

586 Ibid.

587 Avraham and Yuracko (2017).

The last argument proposed by Avraham and Yuracko is linked to trade-offs between efficiency and fairness.[588] In particular, they identify three arguments on the basis of which efficiency should not be the only criterion for the establishment of damages. First, as most people value fairness, one could think giving fairness lexical priority in the social welfare function is an argument.[589] The problem with this argument is that some people would not agree with always giving lexical priority to fairness over efficiency.[590] Second, rule utilitarianism may dictate avoiding targeting even if in some circumstances it would be better not doing so.[591] According to rule utilitarianism, it is better to follow rules that generally lead to higher social welfare than to try to establish in each single occasion which of a set of actions will lead to the highest social welfare. In this view, avoiding targeting might generally lead to higher social welfare if, for instance, this practice could undermine social cohesion.[592] Yet, the rule utilitarianism argument is limited in two ways:[593] first, whether avoiding targeting generally leads to higher social welfare is an empirical question. Rule utilitarianism may actually target at disadvantaged individuals (for instance, if indeed their contribution to society is extremely limited).[594] Second, contrary to traditional law and economic wisdom, sometimes it might be better to address inequalities via private law than via the tax and transfer system.[595] For instance, this is the case when relying on the former is more expensive than acting via tax law. Yet, as Avraham and Yuracko themselves recognize, this is unlikely to be the case with regards to the choice between employing blended and non-blended tables.[596] Indeed, both types of tables are freely available, thus, not costly to adopt for the establishment of damages.

In sum, existing literature has so far highlighted various arguments according to which law and economics should not support the use of non-blended tables. Yet, as recognized by the same literature, none of these arguments is necessarily fatal to the traditional view according to which the use of blended tables is unwarranted.

588 Ibid.
589 Ibid.
590 Ibid.
591 Ibid.
592 Ibid.
593 Ibid.
594 Ibid.
595 Ibid.
596 Ibid.

5.6 A Behavioral Perspective of the Use of Blended vs Non-Blended Tables

In the following I elaborate on the ideas put forward by Avraham and Yuracko and show that some of the arguments they propose are stronger when the neoclassical analysis is complemented with a behaviorally informed one. In particular, I will draw insights from studies on the outgroup homogeneity bias, willingness to accept (WTA), willingness to pay (WTP), gap and anchoring.

5.6.1 Outgroup Homogeneity Bias and Non-Blended Tables

As discussed in the previous section, one of the reasons why the use of non-blended tables may decrease the efficiency of tort law systems compared to blended tables is that the former might be less accurate as they may fail to capture the variability of socioeconomic indicators within different racial groups. While it is certainly true that these tables do not report the variance of the measures, the main weakness of this argument is that the same holds for blended tables. Consequently, it is impossible from a theoretical perspective to know which type of table will generally lead to a higher underestimation of the variance in the measure considered. The main contention of this section is that behavioral economics support the idea that the use of non-blended tables is likely to ease the systematic underestimation of the variance within the racial/gender group that is the least represented in the judiciary. In addition, I will argue that this systematic underestimation may lead to decreases in social welfare. The arguments proposed here are based on studies on the outgroup homogeneity bias. I will start by briefly introducing this bias. Subsequently, I will apply these insights to the use of tables in tort trials.

The outgroup homogeneity bias refers to the phenomenon by which individuals tend to perceive the members of groups with which they do not identify as being: i) more homogeneous than they really are; ii) more homogeneous than the group to which the individual belongs.[597] Given that in the present section I focus mainly on accuracy, in the following sections I will refer to the effect of this bias only in terms of the first effect described above.

---

597 Charles Judd et al., 2005. Attributions of Intergroup Bias and Outgroup Homogeneity to Ingroup and Outgroup Others, 35 EUR. J. SOC. PSYCHOL. 677.

In the context of this strand of literature, a group can be any type of group, from groups artificially created in the lab (e.g. individuals wearing blue or red t-shirts) to social groups, such as gender, ethnicity or race.[598] Existing research indicates that this phenomenon is robust and that the strength of this bias depends on various factors.[599] For instance, the size of the outgroup moderates bias. In particular, ceteris paribus, the larger the size of the outgroup, the larger the bias. In addition, the bias is moderated by the actual variability of the outgroup. The less the actual variability, the smaller the bias. Similarly, the perceived homogeneity of groups is stronger when the evaluation is carried out on the basis of a stereotypical trait.[600] Last, but not least, bias seems to be generally stronger when the observer's socioeconomic status is higher than the one of the outgroup members'.[601] More importantly, it has been shown that a social status effect also takes place in the context of evaluating the heterogeneity of racial minorities.[602]

The outgroup homogeneity bias has been shown to have a strict and self-reinforcing link with the behavior of the observer. In particular, building on existing psychological evidence, Alter and Darley have shown that the perceived homogeneity of a group is positively related to collective treatment of the group.[603] In other words, the more we perceive a group to be homogeneous, the more we tend to behave uniformly towards the individuals belonging to this group.[604] Importantly, this effect has been shown with regards to the allocation of punishment and rewards.[605] In turn, the collective treatment of the group reinforces the perceived homogeneity of the group, potentially leading to a vicious circle.[606] In this

---

598 Alberto Voci, 2000. Perceived Group Variability and the Salience of Personal and Social Identity, 11 EUR. R. OF SOC. PSYCHOL. 177; Mark Rubin et al., 2001. Stretching the Boundaries: Strategic Perceptions of Intragroup Variability. 31 EUR. J. OF SOC. PSYCHOL. 413.

599 Jennifer Boldry et al. 2007. Measuring the Measures a Meta-Analytic Investigation of the Measures of Outgroup Homogeneity, 10 GROUP PROCESSES & INTERGROUP REL. 157.

600 Mark Rubin and Constantina Badea, 2012. They're All the Same!... but for Several Different Reasons: A Review of the Multicausal Nature of Perceived Group Variability, 21 CURRENT DIRECTIONS IN PSYCHOL. SCI. 367.

601 Ibid.

602 Ibid.

603 Adam Alter and John Darley, 2009. When the Association Between Appearance and Outcome Contaminates Social Judgment: A Bidirectional Model Linking Group Homogeneity and Collective Treatment, 97, J. OF PERS. AND SOC. PSYCHOL. 776.

604 Ibid.

605 Ibid.

606 Ibid.

connection, various strands of research indicate that perceived group homogeneity fosters higher punishments for actions (e.g. crimes) committed by individuals belonging to that group.[607]

When applied to the use of statistical tables in the context of tort law, the literature on outgroup homogeneity bias suggests that adjudicators may have a systematically biased perception of the variability of outgroup members in terms of the measures captured by the tables. In fact, psychological research indicates that outgroup homogeneity bias is triggered in situations where the personal identity of the target individual (in a tort law case, the victim) is made salient in a subtle way.[608] Indeed, the use of non-blended tables enhances in a subtle way the saliency of the racial/gender group to which the victim belongs, and thus potentially triggers the bias. In legal systems in which courts have (and make use of their) discretion to adapt damage awards depending on the specific circumstances of the case, the use of non-blended tables may therefore lead to systematic biases in the estimation of damages across groups of victims. To illustrate, imagine a society composed of two groups (X;Y). A judge that belongs to group X is called to award damages for loss of future earning capacity of a victim of a tort. If damages are established on the basis of blended tables, the bias is not triggered. This applies especially in all those cases in which the race of the victims would remain otherwise unknown to the judge, such as proceedings in which parties do not appear in front of the court. Conversely, the use of non-blended tables will trigger the bias, thus, lead to forecast future losses for members of the group Y without taking into account the actual variability within this group. Notice that this could repeatedly occur in the establishment of damages, making it a non-trivial issue. For instance, the bias could be triggered both when the damage is calculated on the basis of these tables and subsequently when it is adapted to the specific circumstance of the victim (e.g. considering gender/race based relative mortality ratios based on smoking habits).

The degree by which the underestimation of the variability of the losses suffered by individuals belonging to a certain racial or gender group occurs depends on the demographic composition of the judiciary within a legal system. Judiciaries

607 Anna-Kaisa Newheiser et al. 2012. Why Do We Punish Groups? High Entitativity Promotes Moral Suspicion, 48, J. OF EXPERIMENTAL SOC. PSYCHOL. 931.

608 Voci (2000).

in the Western world are predominantly composed of White individuals.[609] This seems to be particularly true for European judiciaries.[610] This suggests that it is the variance of the losses suffered by members of racial minority groups that are more likely to be systematically miss-estimated. The fact that outgroup homogeneity bias is particularly strong towards minorities and given the self-reinforcing effect of collective treatment, it is plausible that this effect is not negligible.

Shifting the attention towards gender groups, here the bias is likely to be less systematic in several legal systems. In fact, in many Western judiciaries, gender gap is not large. Sometimes women are the majority of judges sitting in lower courts.[611] Yet, this only implies that the underestimation of the variability of the socioeconomic measure considered will occur for both groups, just in a less systematic manner.

What are the welfare effects of the use of non-blended tables? Generally, from a law and economics perspective damages awards should be set equal to the actual harm suffered by victims.[612] Yet, for optimal prevention to take place what matters is only average accuracy.[613] Changes in the perceived variability of the harm suffered by outgroup members do not necessarily lead to changes in the perceived average harm inflicted to this group. In this sense, the outgroup homogeneity bias may not have welfare implications. Nonetheless, recent law and economics scholarship has highlighted that the homogeneity bias can sometimes lead to decreases in social welfare.[614] In particular, this occurs when courts impose liability under a negligence rule in a situation in which multiple victims are involved.[615] For instance, imagine that a court has to establish whether to make a

609 The proportion of racial minority judges and female judges in the US varies across states, indicating that the outgroup homogeneity bias is likely to be more of a problem in some state than in others. For instance, in 2008 there were no judges that belonged to a racial minority in the state courts of six US states (Maine, Montana, New Hampshire, South Dakota, Vermont, and Wyoming), while in New York the percentage of minority judges was 20.5%. See Malia Reddick et al., 2009. Racial and Gender Diversity on State Courts, 48 THE JUDGES' J. 1.

610 See, for instance, a study conducted on behalf of the Dutch judiciary, indicating that judges with non-European ancestry are very few. Böcker and de Groot-van Leeuwen (2007).

611 Vincenzo Ferrari, 2006. Diritto E Societa: Elementi Di Sociologia Del Diritto, LATERZA & FIGLI SPA.

612 Louis Kaplow and Steven Shavell, 1996. Accuracy in the Assessment of Damages, 39 J. OF L. & ECON. 191.

613 Ibid.

614 Halbersberg and Guttel (2014).

615 Ibid.

tortfeasor (A) liable for some losses suffered by B and C.[616] The expected harm suffered by B and C is respectively 60 and 10.[617] While their cost of precautions is 30 and 50 respectively.[618] If the precautionary costs of the tortfeasor were 50 and the judge does not distinguish the different losses/costs sustained by single victims, A would be made liable. Indeed, she could have avoided a loss of 70 by investing 50.[619] However, the opposite result would be obtained if judges were able to distinguish the specific situation of each victim.[620] In this scenario, B would invest 30 to avoid the loss of 50, while C would prefer to bear the loss of 10.[621] In this situation the total cost of the accident is 40, which is lower than the one we would have if A was made liable.[622] The use of non-blended tables may, therefore, lead to decreases in social welfare. Since the bias would be triggered less frequently if blended tables were used, this negative welfare consequence of adjudication would be a less compelling problem.

To sum up, this section has argued that the employment of non-blended tables may trigger the outgroup homogeneity bias. In turn, this bias may decrease the efficiency of tort law systems by exposing tortfeasors to either a too high or a too low expected liability.

5.6.2 WTA-WTP Gap and Non-Blended Tables

As mentioned above, the third critique moved by Avraham and Yuracko to the employment of non-blended tables relates directly to the use of peoples' WTP for establishing the right amount of safety measures to be taken. While Avraham's argument is mainly grounded in non-welfarist considerations, the present section argues that behavioral economics provides arguments in favor of using the WTA measure. This, in turn, strengthens the case for the use of blended tables.

In principle, the evaluation of positive and negative changes in welfare linked to the consequence of an action (e.g. investing in safety measures) could be conducted on the basis of the WTP or the WTA of the individuals involved. Standard

---

616 Ibid.

617 Ibid.

618 Ibid.

619 Ibid.

620 Ibid.

621 Ibid.

622 Ibid.

economic theory employs WTP under the assumption that the two measures provide very similar values (net of the potential effect of income and wealth).[623] A number of studies have shown that this assumption often does not correspond to reality. Indeed, a substantial amount of research in psychology and behavioral economics has identified systematic divergences between the two measures, with WTA being much larger than WTP.[624] An earlier review found that WTA/WTP ratio to be 7.17 and a more recent one 3.28.[625] Scholars interested in cost-benefit analysis have long discussed the implications of the choice of the best measure to be used in cost-benefit analysis.[626] While consensus is far from being reached,[627] the practice of evaluating policies solely on the basis of WTP is not anymore an obvious choice. Of particular interest for the present article is that research on the WTA/WTP gap highlights that gains and losses are often not evaluated in absolute terms, but in terms of variations that occur starting from a reference point (for instance, but not necessarily, the status quo).[628] As explained by Knetsch, this reference dependence implies that positive changes can be either gains (in the domain of gains, meaning when there is a potential welfare improvement compared to the status quo) or reductions of losses (if the domain is that of losses, i.e. when there is a potential reduction in welfare compared to the reference point). Conversely, a negative change is either a foregone gain (in the domain of gains) or a loss (in the domain of losses).[629] According to Knetsch, WTA is the most appropriate measure to evaluate reductions in losses and the WTP is the most suitable to measure foregone gains.[630] This is because these two measures are those that would bring the victim to the same situation in which she was before the accident.[631] Notice that also this firm view does not provide a clear answer to whether

623 Jack Knetsch, 2015. The Curiously Continuing Saga of Choosing the Measure of Welfare Changes, 6 J. BENEFIT COST ANALYSIS 217.

624 See John Horowitz and Kenneth McConnell, 2002. A Review of WTA/WTP Studies, 44 J. ENVTL. ECON. & MGMT. 426; Tuba Tunçela and James Hammitt, 2014. A New Meta-analysis on the WTP/WTA Disparity, 68 J. ENVTL. ECON. & MGMT. 175.

625 Horowitz and McConnell (2015); Tunçela and Hammitt (2014).

626 Compare Knetsch (2015); and Thomas Kniesner et al., 2014. Willingness to Accept Equals Willingness to Pay for Labor Market Estimates of the Value of a Statistical Life, 48 J. RISK & UNCERTAINTY 187.

627 Knetsch (2015).

628 Ibid.

629 Ibid.

630 Ibid.

631 Ibid.

optimal care in a tort law context should be determined considering victims' WTA or WTP. In fact, it is not clear, for instance, whether victims perceive a loss in earning capacity as a forgone gain or a loss (that could be reduced). Yet, this literature is relevant for the present discussion because it weakens the case for the use of WTP in tort law contexts and provides an alternative measure that could be used instead. Notice that if WTA is adopted, tortfeasors would be generally required to take more precautionary measures and/or decrease more of their activity level compared to a state of the world in which cost-benefit analysis is based on WTP. Thus, it is possible that in the current state of affairs the social cost of several human activities is too high.

In addition, a major difference between WTP and WTA is that the latter is not constrained by wealth. For this reason, when compared with WTP, WTA is more likely to vary less across individuals with different levels of wealth.[632] As a consequence, using WTA instead of WTP is often seen as a practice that would lead to a more equitable distribution of hazards.[633] As highlighted above, a more equal distribution of tort losses across racial and gender groups would be achieved if damages were calculated using blended tables than otherwise. In this sense, the employment of blended tables may better approximate the result that would be achieved had WTA been adopted. Indeed, under both regimes (blended tables and WTA), the distribution of losses across social groups would be more homogeneous than if non-blended tables or WTP were employed. Whether this is in fact the case is an empirical question which the present article cannot answer. Yet, once this possibility is considered, it is not any more obvious that the employment of non-blended tables will necessarily lead to welfare improvements compared to the use of blended ones. In particular, this would depend on whether: (i) WTA is a better measure for the cost-benefit analysis in the realm of tort law; (ii) which type of tables better approximate WTA.

In addition, since the employment of blended tables would reduce the burden suffered by members of disadvantaged groups, their use may lead to better spreading of losses. Loss spreading is widely recognized as the secondary goal of tort law,[634] and refers to the optimal allocation of the risk of losses given the risks

---

632 William Breffle et al., 2015. Understanding How Income Influences Willingness to Pay for Joint Programs: A More Equitable Value Measure for the Less Wealthy, 109 ECOLOGICAL ECON. 17.

633 Ibid.

634 Calabresi (1970).

preferences of victims and tortfeasors.[635] Generally, loss spreading leads to higher levels of social utility when risk-averse individuals bear lower expected losses.[636] For a risk-averse individual (as most humans are), the marginal utility of money decreases for any increase in wealth.[637] This is because the reduction in utility that derives from a certain financial loss is greater than the increase in utility that follows a gain of an equal amount.[638]

It is generally agreed in the literature that the decrease in utility due to a loss that risk-averse individuals experience is positively correlated with the size of the loss relative to the personal wealth. In other words, the larger the loss relative to the assets of a risk-averse person, the greater the decrease in utility suffered.[639] For this reason, a redistribution of expected losses from the less privileged to the most affluent members of a society, as would happen if blended tables were used instead of non-blended ones, may sometimes increase social welfare.

To sum up, in this section I have argued that the literature on the WTP/WTA gap supports the employment of blended tables in three ways: (1) it generally weakens the case for the use of WTP measures in tort law; (2) to the extent that WTA has to be considered the right measure, it is not clear anymore whether non-blended tables are superior to blended ones in terms of social welfare maximization. The fact that the employment of WTA leads to more equitable distribution of losses across social groups suggests that the use of blended tables may better approximate the result that would be obtained if WTA was used as a measure; (3) when read in conjunction with the literature on loss spreading, it seems that the use of blended tables may also generate welfare benefits by leading to a more equitable redistribution of losses.

5.6.3 Anchoring and Non-Blended Tables

In the previous section, I have highlighted how the group homogeneity bias and the WTA-WTP gap can support the claim that blended tables are indeed more appropriate to establish damages in tort trials. In this section, I expand the

635 Shavell (2004)

636 As mentioned above, risk-averse individuals are those that dislike being exposed to pure financial risk.

637 Shavell (2004).

638 Ibid.

639 Ibid.

behavioural-informed analysis of the employment of non-blended tables in tort trials by looking at a widely studied phenomenon: anchoring and adjustment. I argue that, given the existence of this phenomenon, the use of non-blended tables is even less warranted than otherwise.

Anchoring and adjustment refers to the phenomenon by which individuals make evaluations that are biased by irrelevant information (the anchor).[640] For instance, in a classical experiment on anchoring and adjustment, individuals provided systematically different estimates of the percentage of African countries that are part of the United Nations depending on whether they were previously exposed to one of two numbers that were manifestly irrelevant for the completion of the task.[641] Research indicates that this phenomenon is due to the fact that individuals' judgement is initially affected by the anchor and the following adjustment (which is logically warranted given the irrelevance of the information) is not sufficient to avoid the contamination.[642]

Legal scholarship is familiar with the existence of this bias.[643] Indeed, this bias has been replicated with US and EU judges.[644] In addition, this effect has been found both with regards to numeric judgments as well as concerning judgments of ambiguous legal standards.[645] This phenomenon is therefore of clear relevance for the study of judicial decision-making. In the context of the present article, anchoring is a relevant phenomenon because statistical tables can provide an anchor for the establishment of other typologies of damages and spread even further inequalities in awards between social groups.

Legal systems provide different taxonomies of damages. As illustrated above, depending on the country considered, gender and race-based tables are used to calculate one or more types of damages, but not others. For instance, as illustrated above, under English, French, Italian, and US law statistical tables are used for determining the losses of future earning capacity. In this context, their use might

---

640 Tversky and Kahneman (1974).

641 Ibid.

642 Ibid.

643 See, for instance, Yuval Feldman et al., 2016. Anchoring Legal Standards, 13(2) J. EMPIR. LEG. STUD 298.

644 Chris Guthrie et al. 2000. Inside the Judicial Mind, 86 CORNELL L. REV. 777, 792; Jeffrey Rachlinski et al. 2015. Can Judges Make Reliable Numeric Judgments: Distorted Damages and Skewed Sentences, 90 IND. L. J. 695, 730.

645 Feldman et al. (2016).

be warranted because work life expectancy is indeed a relevant factor to establish the likely amount that the subject would have earned had the accident not occurred.

Yet, imagine if the estimation of these losses would provide an anchor for the determination of economic damages that the victim had to bear as a consequence of the accident. This could occur, for instance, with regards to goods for which the market value does not correspond to a specific sum a judge can reference, but to a range from which the judge, with some discretion, picks a number. This occurs, for instance, when economic damages are established in the abstract. An example of a determination of damages at an abstract level is material harm to cars.[646] Here, for instance, the damage is assessed by considering the cost that a mechanic would charge to repair the car, regardless of whether the reparation actually takes place.[647] Notice that many goods belong to this category, as there is no exact market value with regards to houses, used cars (by definition any car that circulates is a used one), and data stored in hardware, for instance. For damages aimed at compensating these types of losses, the influence of the tables has a less obvious justification.

How is this discussion related to the use of (non-)blended tables? The starting point of the analysis is that regardless of whether one uses blended or non-blended tables, anchoring can affect the decision of the judge.[648] However, the effect of the anchor is likely to be different depending on the type of table used. In fact, contrary to blended tables, non-blended ones are likely to provide different anchors and therefore lead to different estimation of damages across racial and gender groups. In particular, social groups that are disadvantaged by the employment of these tables will be further penalized by the bias, since their damages awards for type of damages unrelated to socioeconomic status would be relatively lower than those of non-disadvantaged individuals. This can spread social inequalities beyond what is warranted by the conventional law and economics view of the use of statistical tables. In fact, the lower anchors provided by the tables for victims who are members of disadvantaged racial and gender groups might bias the estimation of the other types of damages downwards compared to the anchor provided by members

646 Michael Faure and Louis Visscher, 2011. The Role of Experts in Assessing Damages–A Law and Economics Account, 2 EUR. J. RISK REG. 376.

647 Ibid.

648 Notice that effect of anchoring may also change the expectations of the victim. However, since I focus on unilateral accidents here, the attention is on the decision of the judge and the incentives to tortfeasors.

of advantaged groups. This type of disparity in damage awards would not occur if blended tables provide the anchor.

What are the potential welfare effects of the use of non-blended tables? As argued above, when courts establish damages on the basis of non-blended tables, anchoring has the effect of redistributing resources from disadvantaged groups towards advantaged ones. This redistribution would occur beyond what standard law and economic analysis suggests. Because of this redistribution, anchoring makes it unclear which policy regime (blended vs. non-blended tables approach) would benefit social welfare more. The answer to this question remains an empirical one, which goes beyond the aim of the present article. The following are two theoretical arguments that suggest that social welfare is likely to be higher in the presence of anchoring if blended tables are used.

The first argument relates to loss spreading. As discussed above, loss spreading suggests exercising care in setting up a tort law system that redirects expected losses from relatively wealthy individuals to the relatively disadvantaged ones. An anchor-based on blended tables does not disfavor any of the social groups, while anchoring relative to non-blended tables further increase losses suffered by members of economically disadvantaged groups. Because of this, when anchoring is considered, non-blended tables may lead to lower social welfare states compared to blended ones.

The starting point of the second argument is that neoclassical economics is not per se against policies that increase equality. As long as members of a society have a preference for fairness, mainstream law and economics accept the incorporation of distributive justice concerns into the social welfare function.[649] As noted by Avraham, this fact provides an argument in favor of the use of blended tables, but only under the condition that in this society there is a sufficient number of individuals that are neither sexists nor racists, or believe that welfare maximization always trumps inequality regardless of whether this inequality is a product of discrimination.[650] Starting from these premises, literature on anchoring overcomes the limit highlighted by Avraham.

As discussed above, in presence of anchoring, it is unclear which of the two policy choices would yield higher social welfare, even though the loss-spreading

---

649 Louis Kaplow and Steven Shavell, 2003. Fairness Versus Welfare: Notes on the Pareto Principles, Preferences, and Distributive Justice, 32 J. LEG. STUD 331.

650 Avraham and Yuracko (2017).

argument points in favor of the use of blended tables. Because of this, a strict welfarist cannot have strong preferences in favor of one of the two options. Thus, the chances that a society would support the use of non-blended tables is much smaller in presence of anchoring than otherwise. This possibility is further reduced when one considers a person could support the use of blended tables only when his or her preferences are sufficiently strong, that s/he would prefer a legal system that worsens the position of minority groups and women to an extent that has no connection with any logical argument. The effect of anchoring on the determination of damages for which tables should not be used is foreign to any logic (e.g. for material harm to cars), as explained above This, in turn, may further reduce the strength of the argument against the use of blended tables.

In a nutshell, the effect of anchoring on the determination of damages is likely to foster social inequalities to an extent that is not justified from a logical or welfarist perspective. In addition, it is likely to increase the losses suffered by members of disadvantaged groups, thus leading to less efficient loss spreading. Furthermore, the illogic and potentially welfare-decreasing effect of anchoring should reduce the support that blended tables can find in a given society. To the extent that individual preferences for fairness should be considered in the welfare function of a society, the standard law and economics argument against the use of blended tables is less tenable than usually assumed.

This section has taken a behavioral approach to the study of the welfare effects related to the employment of (non-) blended tables in tort trials. Overall, the analysis has shown that various strands of literature suggest that the employment of non-blended tables compared to the use of blended ones may lead to decreases in social welfare. Therefore, the welfarist case for the use of non-blended tables is much weaker than usually assumed in law and economics. This analysis complements and supports the recent claim put forward by Avraham and Yuracko that the use of non-blended tables in tort trials is unfair and inefficient. In the remainder of this article I elaborate on how to address these concerns.

5.7 Conclusion

The US courts' practice to employ gender and race based statistical tables for the assessment of tort law damages has been heavily criticized in the recent past. While earlier criticisms came mainly from the perspective of distributive justice, recent scholarship has argued that this practice is (and/or should be) against the achievement of corrective justice and efficiency.

The present work has built upon and expanded this literature from two perspectives. First, given how controversial the use of these tables is, I have analysed whether similar practices take place under European tort law. More specifically I have focused on three major European jurisdictions: England, France and Italy. The analysis has shown that these European courts do not differentiate between racial groups in the employment of statistical tables. In addition, the role of gender is generally more limited in these two jurisdictions than in the US. This is especially true with regards to the Italian legal system.

Second, as explicitly recognized by this literature, the welfarist case against the use of these tables in tort trials has various weaknesses. The present work has expanded the welfare analysis by taking a behavioral perspective on the issue. On this ground it has been argued that the welfarist case for the use of non-blended tables is weaker than generally assumed.

Overall this study suggests that the employment of non-blended tables in tort trials may reduce social welfare. As such, even from a pure welfarist perspective, it might be abandoned in favour of blended tables. In this connection, the English, the French and the Italian practice seem to be more in line with this recommendation than the US one.

6 Accuracy and Discrimination at Trial: Putting the Pieces Together

6.1 Main Findings

The core issue addressed in this book is the interplay between accuracy and the behavioral economics of evidence law in tort trials. The topic has been touched upon at various points and from different perspectives throughout the various Chapters. In this Chapter, I will bring this work to a synthesis, with the aim to contribute to three streams of literature on accuracy and behavioral law and economics.

The first stream of literature is concerned with whether behavioral law and economics can increase our understanding of human behavior vis-à-vis neoclassical law and economics. The second focuses on whether behavioral law and economics suggests that we should trust less courts' ability to make accurate decisions at trial. The last one focuses on whether behavioral law and economics provides arguments to review the central role that accuracy in adjudication has within contemporary legal scholarship. After having elaborated how this book relates to each of these three strands of literature, I present some suggestions on how this work could be expanded.

6.2 The Interplay Between Accuracy and Behavioral Law and Economics

The first issue I discuss is whether integrating economic insights with behavioral ones improves our ability to predict how certain legal rules and institutions affect behavior. The analysis shows that a behavioral approach can provide a useful complement to neoclassical economics in describing the behavior of judges and other trial participants and thus the functioning of tort law systems.

This complementing role is in Chapter 4, where I discuss the relevance of IRBs in tort trials. The analysis shows that these biases may affect the evaluation of different types of items of evidence (and thus, ultimately, tort trial outcomes) in a predictable manner. In particular, implicit biases may reduce the expected benefit for members of discriminated racial minorities to bring a case to trial. As a consequence of this, minority members may be exposed to a higher degree of

G. Dominioni, *Biased Trials*, Ökonomische Analyse des Rechts | Economic Analysis of Law, https://doi.org/10.1007/978-3-658-30080-7_6

expected liability as well as of negative externalities than in absence of the bias. In other words, via tort law, implicit biases may shift the expected distribution of resources from one racial group to another, to the advantage of members of non-discriminated groups. This shift may distort the deterrent effect of tort law depending on the expected distribution of the harm across different populations of victims. In this connection, I argue that there is a positive correlation between the proportion of the expected harm suffered by members of racial minorities and the decrease in the deterrent effect of tort law. In addition, the Chapter has discussed various policies that could be implemented to address these distortive effects. In this connection, careful attention towards human cognition and motivation can provide precious insights on which policies are likely to be more effective.

On a related note, Chapter 5 discusses the welfare effects of the use of blended vs non-blended (i.e. race/gender based) statistical tables for the compensation of future losses in tort trials. Also here, taking a behavioral perspective has shown to provide guidance to policymakers regarding the effects of this important tort law practice on judges and tortfeasors' behavior. An overall result of the book is that, in the context of European judiciaries, the behavioral phenomena considered here all point into the direction that members of racial minorities are likely to be impaired in their ability to obtain compensation at trial. In this sense, behavioral economics may be able to provide policymakers with insights on the functioning of tort law systems in Europe.

While behavioral insights can be relevant for policymaking, this work has also shown that legal scholars should be careful in complementing law and economics with behavioral studies to inform the law. Chapter 2 has warned against some problem that derive from the misuse of behavioral findings to inform policymaking. In particular, the issue addressed in this Chapter is that legal scholarship that uses findings from behavioral sciences to evaluate the performance of trial systems pay sometimes too little attention to differences in truth standards adopted in studies on JDM. This lack of attention can create confusion regarding why, whether, and under what circumstances a behavioral phenomenon can be considered problematic and, if so, what are the appropriate policies that could be adopted to address these concerns.

In a similar vein, the experiment performed in Chapter 3 provides support to the claim that legal scholars should be careful in translating findings obtained with laypeople to describe the behavior of judges. In particular, the Chapter has highlighted that individuals enrolled in a school that prepares to become judges are less prone to commit the FAE in trial settings than law students when this error is triggered by contextual factors (i.e. character evidence). Yet, the Chapter has also shown that when the FAE is triggered by individual propensities the two groups do not differ. This indicates that making parallels between expert and non-expert is sometimes warranted. These findings highlight the potential of behavioral law and economics to complement neoclassical studies in understanding how judges make decisions.

The second main issue addressed in this book is whether, once behavioral insights are taken into account, we should be more skeptical of the accuracy of courts' decisions. Accuracy in adjudication is often seen as a major criterion to evaluate the performance of trial systems. This is true also from a law and economics perspective, for instance, when accuracy refers to the imposition of liability. The analysis has highlighted mixed results. On the one hand, various strands of research in behavioral law and economics indicate that human decision-making is sometimes inaccurate. In this regard, Chapter 2 and 3 discuss the role of the FAE in trial settings. Building on existing literature, Chapter 2 highlights that the FAE may reduce the accuracy of courts in the imposition of liability. This hypothesis found support in Chapter 3, where it was shown that individuals with a background in law are likely to commit this error when they have a predisposition to do so. In addition, Chapter 5 has argued that the use of non-blended statistical tables in trial settings may trigger the outgroup homogeneity bias, according to which individuals underestimate the variance in a certain characteristic of outgroup members. Overall, these arguments point in the direction that indeed behavioral study should make us wary of fully trusting the accuracy of courts' decisions.

Despite these general results, the book has also highlighted that determining whether a particular behavioral phenomenon is likely to increase or decrease the accuracy of court's decisions is often more difficult than assumed in a large part of the literature in behavioral law and economics. There are various reasons why this is the case.

i) Some behavioral phenomena are not evaluable in terms of accuracy, and therefore do not offer any hint regarding whether the outcome of a trial is likely to be more or less accurate depending on whether they are influenced by them. This is the case, for instance with implicit racial attitudes, which are evaluable from a correspondence perspective.

ii) Behavioral phenomena that highlight errors in the way information is processed offer only limited help to understand whether courts' accuracy is improved or decreased by their influence. A bias of this type in the context of adjudication is discussed in Chapter 5, where it is argued that anchoring may lead to unequal trial outcomes that go beyond what could be justified on the ground on traditional arguments in law and economics. There it was highlighted that studies on anchoring do not necessarily provide much insights on whether damages awards are made less accurate by this bias. Generally, it can happen that an illogical judgment increases the accuracy of a decision when, for instance, the judgment is made on the basis of inaccurate information. If the setup of procedural rules provides systematically inaccurate information to the judge, a bias may overall increase accuracy.

iii) Since trials are complex and iterative procedures in which trial actors interact with one another, biases that lead to increase accuracy with regards to single judgments made at trial, may decrease the overall accuracy of trial outcomes when, for instance, they impair the information flow between the defendant and the judge.

From this discussion it does not follow that behavioral law and economics cannot provide important insights in evaluating the performance of trial systems from the perspective of accuracy. Instead, it highlights that the issue of accuracy at trial when seen through the lenses of behavioral economics is much more complex than often assumed in legal scholarship. As such, while behavioral studies can inform policymaking, more caution might be warranted in drawing prescriptive conclusions on the basis of behavioral findings related to single phenomena.

The third main issue addressed by this book is whether a behavioral approach to adjudication can inform the debate on what should be the aim of adjudication. In this regard, while accuracy in adjudication is seen as a main instrument to reach social welfare maximization, scholars have long highlighted that the pursue of accuracy without consideration of the costs of achieving it may lead to suboptimal outcomes.[651] The behavioral analysis proposed here shows that the pursue of accuracy in adjudication can lead to suboptimal outcomes even in states of the world

651 Kaplow (2015).

in which increasing accuracy is costless. In particular, I have proposed two examples of this type of situation. First, as highlighted in Chapter 4, even if implicit stereotypes increase the accuracy of trial outcomes, they may still reduce social welfare when the discriminated individual is made liable on the basis of these stereotypes. Second, in the same Chapter I argued that the imposition of liability on the basis of an implicit stereotype does not necessarily reduce the suffering imposed on members of racial minorities that derives from the feeling of being discriminated against. This suffering may reduce the willingness of minority members to bring a case to trial and thus reduce the effectiveness of tort law in reducing the level of negative externalities in a given society.

A fourth, major, yet latent, theme of this book is gender and (especially) racial discrimination in tort trials. This issue has been analyzed here from the perspective of ingroup-outgroup biases such as the FAE, implicit racial biases, and the outgroup homogeneity bias. In addition, the book has highlighted that some biases that strictly speaking are generally unrelated to ingroup-outgroups, can become relevant in the discussion of discriminatory trial outcomes when certain aspects of the trial are considered. This was shown, for instance, in Chapter 5 with regards to the effect of anchoring on courts' decisions in presence of non-blended tables.

This book has highlighted that human cognition and motivation can play a significant role in allocating resources (e.g. money, health, freedom) across racial groups. Given the current composition of European judiciaries, this distribution is likely to be mainly unidirectional, in favor of white individuals. Besides distributive concerns, these transfers are likely to reduce social welfare both from a static and a dynamic perspective. On the one hand, outgoup biases in the judiciary may lead to impose excessive liability on minority groups as well as reduce too much the expected liability of white subjects. In addition, since minority members' reduced access to justice is likely to perpetuate and worsen existing disparities among racial groups, outgroup biases can reduce social welfare from a dynamic perspective, i.e. by discouraging minority members' investments in human capital. These trends are likely to be enhanced by certain procedural rules and practices as well as rules of substantive law. In this connection, Chapter 5 discusses the use of blended vs non-blended tables to establish damages for future losses and Chapter 4 investigates the role of various features of procedural and substantive law such as the way in which decisions are motivated and the vagueness of negligence standards.

The geographical scope of the present inquiry has been Europe and the US. In the US, racial issues have long played a prominent role in policy debates. A similar trend is now observable in Europe. In particular, following recent migratory fluxes from Africa and the Middle East, several European countries are facing the issue of finding adequate strategies to effectively integrate incomers and prevent the rise of social conflicts. As discrimination and segregation occur often along ethnic and racial lines, and as tort law is an important determinant of the creation and distribution of resources within a society,[652] addressing discriminatory outcomes in trial settings is a compelling priority in Europe. In this connection, this book has shown that behavioral studies can offer important insights on how discriminatory outcomes can be avoided in trial settings and on the limits of these interventions. In this connection, Chapter 4 has discussed possible debiasing and insulating strategies to address IRBs. In addition, the same Chapter has highlighted the possibility of using alternative policy instruments to reduce society reliance on a potentially biased tort law system.

6.3 Future Research

This book contributes to the study of evidence law and tort law from a behavioral perspective in multifold ways. As often happens when doing research, this inquiry has opened a new plethora of pathways for future research.

First, this book analyzes various avenues to reduce the effects of implicit biases on trial outcomes. Yet, this analysis could be expanded in various directions. First, a similar analysis could be repeated with regards to the other types of outgroup biases than those that have been discussed here. Second, future research can also contribute to a better understanding of whether, and under which conditions, the debiasing mechanisms discussed above are effective strategies. As shown above, the existing literature has started delving in this direction. Results reached so far are informative, but it is still not clear whether, and to what extent, these interventions are effective in real life settings. For instance, as discussed above, one of the main recommendations to decrease implicit biases among judges relates to increase diversity in judicial bodies. Yet, Rachlinski and co-authors found little

652 On a related note on the role of private law in creating inequalities across social groups see: Sandefur Rebecca 2008. Access to Civil Justice and Race, Class, and Gender Inequality. 34 ANNU. REV. SOCIOL 340.

differences in the pervasiveness of implicit biases between groups of judges coming from jurisdictions with great differences in racial diversity in the judiciary.[653] Further research could explore in more depth the conditions under which policies aimed to reduce implicit discrimination at trial are more likely to succeed.

Second, Chapter 5 has highlighted that behavioral studies may offer a new way of doing comparative research in a functional way. There it has been shown that various institutional arrangements/rules are differently able to affect the emergence of a bias in legally relevant contexts. Indeed, different legal systems may adopt different court practices or embrace diverging styles with regards, for instance, how to motivate a decision or on the level of scrutiny that a higher court has on decision of lower courts. This type of research could be of high value for scholars interested in behavioral analysis of law. In fact, two major problems related to implementing debiasing/insulating techniques are that: i) these reforms are often expensive; ii) it is often not clear what are the actual advantages brought by these reforms. Here comparative law can be of great help. On the one hand, comparative analysis may help identifying new (maybe cheaper) debiasing/insulating strategies adopted in foreign legal systems. On the other hand, comparative law may fuel the production of new experimental research aimed at isolating differences across institutional arrangements in terms of their effectiveness in combating undesired behavioral phenomena. Note that this approach to study the law is potentially compatible with various normative approaches. In fact, as a behavioral phenomenon might be seen as problematic according to various normative standards, this approach is open, but not restricted, to the efficiency canon. In this sense, it has the potential to become a fruitful ground of debate and collaboration between law and economics scholars and academics that adhere to different schools of thought.

Third, this research can be expanded in various interesting directions also from an empirical perspective. First, the literature on outgroup biases at trial mainly concentrates on blacks (and whites). However, US and other countries are becoming prismatic societies,[654] and therefore more attention should be given to other racial and ethnic groups (e.g. Hispanics and Asians). Moreover, European

---

653 Rachlinski et al. (2009).

654 Dominioni et al. (2018).

scholarship and policymakers could benefit from research conducted on behaviorally based discrimination against Arabs, Eastern Europeans, and Roma people.[655] Studying ethnic and racial group interactions in trial settings in prismatic societies may require to adopt methods that allow to simultaneously capture interactions among these groups. Some types of Lotka-Volterra models allow to do so and have been recently adopted to study racial groups interactions in the US,[656] trust spillovers among national and European institutions,[657] and interactions among stock prices.[658] This method could provide new insights on how racial and ethnic groups interact in tort law and criminal law settings.

In addition, with few exceptions, most studies on outgroup biases in the courtroom have been conducted with students. The field would benefit from having research conducted with professionals involved in trials. Chapter 3 has moved in this direction, but there is still scope for expansion.

Lastly, Chapter 3 has delved into weather self-selection and training received in careers linked to adjudication may lead judges to be less affected by the FAE. Similar studies could be conducted with regards to other biases. This inquiry could be particularly interesting with regards to biases that are at least partially due to cultural or educational factors.

---

[655] Dominioni and Romano (2017).

[656] Dominioni et al. (2018).

[657] Goran Dominioni et al. 2020. Trust Spillovers Among National and European Institutions. EUR. UNION POLITICS, 1.

[658] Goran Dominioni et al. 2019. A Quantitative Study of the Interactions Between Oil price and Renewable Energy Sources Stock Prices. 12.9 ENERGIES 1693.

Bibliography

Abrams, D. S., Bertrand, M., & Mullainathan, S. (2012). Do Judges Vary in Their Treatment of Race?. The Journal of Legal Studies, 41(2), 347;

Ajzen, I., and Fishbein, M., (1975). A Bayesian Analysis of Attribution Processes, 82(2) Psychological Bulletin, 261;

Alter, A. L., & and Darley, J. M., (2009). When the Association Between Appearance and Outcome Contaminates Social Judgment: A Bidirectional Model Linking Group Homogeneity and Collective Treatment. 97(5) Journal of Personality and Social Psychology, 776;

Avraham R., (2006). Putting a Price on Pain-and-Suffering Damages: A Critique of the Current Approaches and a Preliminary Proposal for Change, 100(1) Northwestern University Law Review 87;

Avraham, R., and Yuracko, K., (2017). Torts and Discrimination, 78.3 Ohio State Law Journal,16;

Bowers, K. S., (1973). Situationism in Psychology: An Analysis and a Critique. 80(5) Psychological Review, 307;

Bagenstos, S., (2007). Implicit Bias, "Science" and Anti-Discrimination Law, 1 Harvard Law Review, 1;

Bauman, C. W., and Skitka L. J., (2010). Making Attributions for Behaviors: The Prevalence of Correspondence Bias in the General Population. 32(3) Basic and Applied Social Psychology 269;

Belton, I. K., Thomson, M., & and Dhami, M. K., (2014). Lawyer and Nonlawyer Susceptibility to Framing Effects in Out-of-Court Civil Litigation Settlement. 11(3) Journal of Empirical Legal Studies, 11(3), 578-600;

Benforado, A., & Hanson, J. D., (2008). The Great Attributional Divide: How Divergent Views of Human Behavior are Shaping Legal Policy. 57 Emory Law Journal, 8;

Berry, J. W., (2002). Cross-cultural Psychology: Research and Applications. Cambridge University Press;

Bhopal R.S., (2007). Racism in Health and Health Care in Europe: Reality or Mirage? 17(3) The European Journal of Public Health 238;

G. Dominioni, *Biased Trials*, Ökonomische Analyse des Rechts | Economic Analysis of Law, https://doi.org/10.1007/978-3-658-30080-7

Blair I.V., et al., (2014). An Investigation of Associations Between Clinicians' Ethnic or Racial Bias and Hypertention Treatment, Medication Adherence and Blood Pressure Control, 29(7) Journal of General Internal Medicine, 990;

Böcker A., and de Groot-van Leeuwen L., (2007). Ethnic Minorities Representation in the Judiciary: Diversity among Judges in Old and New Countries of Immigration, The Judiciary Quarterly, 22;

Boldry, J. G., Gaertner, L., & Quinn, J., (2007). Measuring the measures Measures a Meta-Analytic Investigation of the Measures of Outgroup Homogeneity. 10(2) Group Processes & Intergroup Relations, 10(2), 157;

Breffle, W. S., et al., (2015). Understanding How Income Influences Willingness to Pay for Joint Programs: A More Equitable Value Measure for the Less Wealthy. 109 Ecological Economics, 109, 17;

Brownstein M., Madva A., and Gawronski B., (2019). What Do Implicit Measures Measure? Wiley Interdisciplinary Reviews: Cognitive Science 1501;

Bullard R. D., (2000) Dumping in Dixie: Race, Class, and Environmental Quality Boulder, CO: Westview Press., 3;

Bullard R. D. and Wright B., (2008) Disastrous Response to Natural and Man-Made Disasters: An Environmental Justice Analysis Twenty-Five Years after Warren County, 26 Journal of Environmental Law 217;

Burgess D. J. et al., (2014) The Effect of Cognitive Load and Patient Race on Phyisician's Decisions to Prescribe Opiods for Chronic Low Back Pain: A Randomized Trial, 15 Pain Medicine 965;

Bussani, M., and Infantino, M., (2015). Tort Law and Legal Ccultures. 63(1) American Journal of Comparative Law, 63(1), 77;

Calabresi G., (1970). The Cost of Accidents: A Legal and Economic Analysis. New Haven; London: Yale University Press;

Chamallas, M., and Wriggins, J. B., (2010). The Measure of Iinjury: Rrace, Ggender, and Tort Law. NYU Press;

Cameron C.D., (2012). Sequential Priming Measures of Implicit Social Cognition: A Meta-Analysis of Associations with Behavior and Explicit Attitudes, 16(4) Personality and Social Psychology Review 337;

Cannarsa, M., (2002). Compensation for Personal Injury in France;

Carpenter A. E., (2002). The Hearsay Rule and Racial Evaluations of Credibility 8(1) Washington and Lee Journal of Civil Rights and Social Justice 15;

Casals, M., (2006). 'Children as Victims under the Law of England and Wales', in M. Martin Casals (ed.), Children in Tort Law, Part II: Children as Victims, 68;

Chamallas, M., & Wriggins, J. B., (2010). The Measure of Injury: Race, Gender, and Tort Law. NYU Press;

Chamallas M., (1998). The Architecture of Bias: Deep Structures in Tort Law, 146 University of Pennsylvania Law Review U. PA. L.REV. 463 (January 1998);

Chiu C. et al., (1997). Lay Dispositionism and Implicit Theories of Personality, 73 Journal of Personality and Social Psychology 19;

Choi, I., Nisbett, R. E., and Norenzayan, A., (1999). Causal Attribution Across Cultures: Variation and Universality. 125(1) Psychological Bulletin, 47;

Cintron A., and Morrison R. S., (2006). Pain and Ethnicity in the United States: A Systematic Review, 9 Journal of Palliative Medicine, 1454;

Cooper L. A. et al., (2012). The Associations of Clinicians' Implicit Attitudes About Race With Medical Visit Communication and Patient Ratings of Interpersonal Care, 102(5) American Journal of Public Health, 979;

Comandé G., (2006). Towards a Global Model for Adjudicating Personal Injury Damages: Bridging Europe and the United States, 19(2) Temple International & Comparative Law Journal, 241;

Craig, M. A., and Richeson, J. A., (2014). More Diverse Yet Less Tolerant? How the Increasingly Diverse Racial Landscape Affects white Americans' Racial Attitudes. 40(6) Personality and Social Psychology Bulletin, 750;

Damaška, M., (1997). 49 Truth in Adjudication. Hastings Law Journal289;

Damaška, M. R., (1994). Propensity Evidence in Continental Legal Systems, Chicago-Kent Law Review, Vol. 70, p. 65;

Devine, D. J., and Caughlin, D. E., (2014). Do They Matter? A Meta-Analytic Investigation of Individual Characteristics and Guilt Judgments. 20(2) Psychology, Public Policy, and Law, 116;

Dewees, D., and Trebilcock, M., (1992). The Efficacy of the Tort System and Its Alternatives: A Review of Empirical Evidence. 30 Osgoode Hall Law Journal, 57;

Dewees, D. N., Duff, D., and Trebilcock, M. J., (1996). Exploring the Domain of Accident Law: Taking the Facts Seriously. Oxford University Press on Demand;

De Houwer, J. et al., (2009). Implicit Measures: A Normative Analysis and Review, 135(3) Psychological Bulletin 357;

De Moot, P. B., et al., (2004). The Learned Hand Formula: The Case of the Netherlands, 4(2) Global Jurist Advances, Vol. 4(2);

Di Federico, G., (2005). Recruitment, Professional Evaluation and Career of Judges and Prosecutors in Europe. Istituto di Ricerca Sui Sistemi Giudiziari.

Dominioni, G., and Romano, A., (2017). Trial (Implicit Biases), The Encyclopaedia of Law and Economics, Springer.

Dominioni G., Marasco A., and Romano A., (2018). A Mathematical Approach to Study and Forecast Racial Groups Interactions: Deterministic Modeling and Scenario Method. 52.4 Quality & quantity 1929-1956.

Dominioni G., Romano A., Sotis C., (2019)., A Quantitative Study of the Interactions Between Oil price and Renewable Energy Sources Stock Prices. 12(9) Energies 1693.

Dominioni G., and Heine D., (2019). Behavioural Economics and Public Support for Carbon Pricing: A Revenue Recycling Scheme to Address the Political Economy of Carbon Taxation, 10(3) European Journal of Risk Regulation 554-570.

Dominioni G., Quintavalla A., Romano A., (2020). Trust Spillovers Among National and European Institutions. Eur. Union Politics, 1.

Dominioni G., Desmet P., and Visscher L., (2020). Judges Versus Jurors: Biased Attributions in the Courtroom, 52:1 Cornell International Law Journal, 102.

Dovidio, J., F., et al., (2002). Implicit and Explicit Prejudice and Interracial Interaction 82(1) J Pers Soc Psychol 62;

Dripps, D. A., (2003). Fundamental Retribution Error: Criminal justice and the social psychology of blame. Vand. L. Rev., 56, 1383;

Dubois E., Schurrer C. and Velicogna M., (2013). The Functioning of Judicial Systems and the Situation of the Economy in the European Union Member States;

Dunwoody, P. T., (2009). Dawson, N. V., & Gregory, F. (2009). Correspondence and Coherence in Science: A Brief Historical Perspective. 4(2) Judgment and Decision Making, 126;

Dweck, C. S., Chiu, C. Y., and Hong, Y. Y., (1995). Implicit Theories and Their Role in Judgments and Reactions: A Word from Two Perspectives. 6(4) Psychological Inquiry, 6(4), 267;

Dweck, C. S., (2011). Implicit Theories, in Handbook of Theories of Social Psychology: Collection: 2, 52;

Eberhardt, J. L., (2004). et al Seeing Black: Race, Crime, and Visual Processing, 87 Journal of Personality and Social Psychology 876;

Endler, N. S., and Magnusson, D., (1976). Toward an Interactional Psychology of Personality. 83(5) Psychological Bulletin, 956;

Engel, C., (2013). Behavioral Law and Economics: Empirical Methods, MPI Collective Goods Preprint, No. 2013/1;

EPSC, Legal Migration in the EU 2, (2015);

Epstein, L., Landes, W. M., and Posner, R. A., (2013). The Behavior of Federal Judges: A Theoretical and Empirical Study of Rational Choice. Harvard University Press, 65;

Faigman D. L. et al., (2008). A Matter of Fit: The Law of Discrimination and the Science of Implicit Bias, 59 Hastings Law Journal 1389;

Faure, M. G., (2010). Behavioural Accident Law and Economics. 4 Journal of Applied Economics, 11;

Faure, M., (2015). Private Liability and Critical Infrastructure. 6(2) European Journal of Risk Regulation, 6(2), 229;

Faure, M., and Visscher, L., (2011). The Role of Experts in Assessing Damages–A Law and Economics Account. 2(3) European Journal of Risk Regulation 379;

Fazio, R. H., Jackson, J. R., Dunton, B. C., and Williams, C. J., (1995). Variability in Automatic Activation as an Unobtrusive Measure of Racial Attitudes: A Bona Fide Pipeline? 69(6) Journal of Personality and Social Psychology 1013;

Fazio, R. H., and Olson, M. A., (2003). Implicit Measures in Social Cognition Research: Their Meaning and Use. 54(1) Annual Review of Psychology, 297;

Feldman, Y., et al., (2016). Anchoring Legal Standards. Journal of Empirical Legal Studies, 13(2), 298;

FRA, Inequalities and Multiple Discrimination in Access to and Quality of Healthcare (2013);

Feldman, Y., Schurr, A., and Teichman, D., (2016). Anchoring Legal Standards. 13 Journal of Empirical Legal Studies, 298;

Ferrari, V., (2015). Diritto e Società: Elementi di Sociologia del Diritto. Gius. Laterza & Figli Spa;

Field, Stewart, (2006). State, Citizen, and Character in French Criminal Pocess. 33(4) Journal of Law and Society 33.4, 522;

Funder, D. C., (1987). Errors and Mistakes: Evaluating the Accuracy of Social Judgment, Psychological Bulletin, 101(1);

Galetti, S. C., (2004). The Italian Court Honorary Judges, in Policing in Central and Eastern Europe – Dilemmas of Contemporary Criminal Justice (Gorazd Meško, Milan Pagon, Bojan Dobovšek eds.) Faculty of Criminal Justice University of Maribor 443;

Garoupa N. M., (2012). The Economics of Prosecutors. In: Harel A, K Hylton (eds). Research Handbook on the Economics of Criminal Law. Edward Elgar, Cheltenham, 231;

Garoupa, N., and Rizzolli, M., (2012). Wrongful convictions Convictions Ddo lower Lower Ddeterrence. 168(2) Journal of Institutional and Theoretical Economics, JITE, 168(2), 224-231;

Gazal-Ayal, O., and Sulitzeanu-Kenan, R., (2010). Let My People Go: Ethnic In-Group Bias in Judicial Decisions—Evidence from a Randomized Natural Experiment. 7(3) Journal of Empirical Legal Studies, 403;

Gawronski, B., (2003). Implicational Schemata and the Correspondence Bias: on the Diagnostic Value of Situationally Constrained Behavior. 84(6) Journal of Personality and Social Psychology, 1154;

Gawronski, B., et al., (2008). What Makes Mental Associations Personal or Extrapersonal? Conceptual Issues in the Methodological Debate About Implicit Attitude Measures, 2 Social and Personality Psychology Compass, 1002;

Gazal-Ayal, O., and Sulitzeanu-Kenan, R., (2010). Let My People Go: Ethnic In-Group Bias in Judicial Decisions—Evidence from a Randomized Natural Experiment. 7(3) Journal of Empirical Legal Studies, 403;

Gervey, B. M., et al., (1999). Differential Use of Person Information in Decisions about Guilt Versus Innocence: The Role of Implicit Theories, 25(1) Personality and Social Psychology Bulletin, 26;

Giard, R. W., (2013). Birth-Related Brain Injuries: Torts in Trouble;

Gibson, E., (1993). The Gendered Wage Dilemma in Personal Injury Damages, in Tort Theory 185, 198 (Ken Cooper–Stephenson & Elaine Gibson eds.);

Giesen, I., (2012). Attribution, Legal Causation and Preventive Effects, in Judicial Decision Making in Civil Law, Eleven International Publishing;

Gilbert, D. T., and Malone P. S., (1995). The Correspondence Bias, Psychological Bulletin, 117 (1);

Glaeser, E. L., and Sacerdote B., (2003). Sentencing in Homicide Cases and the Roles of Vengeance, 32 Journal of Legal Studies, 363;

Godsil, R. D., (2012). Environmental Law: a Tale of Two Neighborhoods, Implicit Bias and Environmental Decision Making, in Implicit Racial Biases Accross the Law, Cambridge University Press (Levinson and Smith Eds.), 2012, pp. 192;

Graham, S., and Lowery B. S., (2004). Priming Unconscious Racial Stereotypes About Adolescent Offenders, 28 Law and Human Behavior, 483;

Graziadei, M., (2009). What went wrong? Tort Law, Personal Responsibility, Expectations of Proper Care and Compensation. In European Tort Law. Springer Vienna;

Green, A. R., et al., (2007). Implicit Bias Among Physicians and Its Prediction of Thrombolysis Decisions for Black and White Patients, 22(9) Journal of General Internal Medicine, 1231;

Greenberg, L., (2001). Compensating the Lead Poisoned Child: Proposals for Mitigating Discriminatory Damage Awards, 28 BC Environmental Affairs Law Review, 429;

Greenwald, A. G., and Bajani, M. R., (1995). Implicit Social Cognition: Attitudes, Self-esteem, and Stereotypes, 102 Psychological Review, 8;

Greenwald, A. G., McGhee, D. E., and Schwartz, J. L., (1998). Measuring Individual Differences in Implicit Cognition: the Implicit Association Test.74(6) Journal of Personality and Social Psychology, 1464;

Greenwald, A. G., et al., (2015). Statistically Small Effects of the Implicit Association Test Can HaveSocietally Large Effects 108(4) Journal of Personality and Social Psychology, 553;

Grossman, G., et al., (2016). Descriptive Representation and Judicial Outcomes in Multi-ethnic societies. 60(1) American Journal of Political Science, 44;

Grunewald, R., (2013). Comparing Injustices: Truth, Justice, and the System. 77 Albany. Law. Review, 77, 1139;

Guthrie, C., et al., (2001). Inside the judicial mind. Cornell L. Rev., 86, 777:

Guthrie, C. et al., (2009). The" Hidden Judiciary": An Empirical Examination of Executive Branch Justice, Duke Law Journal, 1517;

Haack, S., (2014). Justice, Truth, and Proof: Not So Simple, After All;

Hamilton, J. T., (1995). Testing for Environmental Racism: Prejudice, Profits, Political Power?, 14(1) Journal of Policy Analysis and Management, 107;

Hewstone, M., et al., (2002). Integroup Bias, 53 Annual Review of Psychology 575;

Hammond, K. R., (1996). Human Judgment and Social Policy: Irreducible Uncertainty, Inevitable Error, Unavailable Injustice, Oxford University Press;

Hanson, J., and McCann, M., (2008). Situationist Torts, 41 Loyola of Los Angeles Law Review, 1359;

Haider, A. H., et al., (2011). Association of Unconscious Race and Social Class Bias with Vignette-based Clinical Assessments by Medical Students, 306 The Journal of the American Medical Association, 942;

Hilton, D., (2013). Causal Explanation: From Social Perception to Knowledge-Based Attribution, in Social Psychology: Handbook of Basic Principles;

Hirsh A. T., et al., (2015). The Interaction of Patient Race, Provider Bias, and Clinical Ambiguity on Pain Management Decisions 16(6) JOP 558;

Hofmann W., (2005). A Meta-Analysis on the Correlation between the Implicit Association Test and Explicit Self-Report Measure, 31(10) Personality and Personal Psychology Bulletin, 1370;

Horowitz, J. K., and McConnell, K. E., (2002). A Rreview of WTA/WTP Sstudies. 44(3) Journal of Eenvironmental Eeconomics and Management, 44(3), 426-447;

Hunt, J. S., (2015). Race, ethnicityEthnicity, and culture Culture in jury Jury Ddecision Mmaking. 11 Annual Review of Law and Social Science Rev Law Soc Sci 11: 269;

Jennings, K. E., (2010). Coherent Attributions with Co-occurring and Interacting Causes, PhD Thesis University of California, Berkeley;

John, J., (2019). The IAT Is Dead, Long Live The IAT: Context-Sensitive Measures of Implicit Attitudes Are Indispensable to Social and Political Psychology. 28(1) Current Directions in Psychological Science, 10;

Jolls, C., (2007). Behavioral law and economics (No. w12879). National Bureau of Economic Research, 10;

Jolls, C., and Sunstein, C., (2006). The Law of Implicit Bias, 94 California Law Review;

Jolls, C., Sunstein, C. R., and Thaler, R., (1998). A Behavioral Approach to Law and Economics. 50 (5) Stanford Law Review, 1471;

Jones, E. E., and Harris, V. A., (1967). The Attribution of Attitudes. 3(1) Journal of Experimental Social Psychology, 1;

Jost, J. T. et al., (2009). The Existence of Implicit Bias is Beyond Reasonable Doubt: A Refutation of Ideological and Methodological Objections and Executive Summary of Ten Studies that No Manager Should Ignore, 29 Research in Organizational Behavior, 39;

Judd, et al., (2005). Attributions of Intergroup Bias and Outgroup Homogeneity to Ingroup and Outgroup Others, 35 European Journal of Social Psychology, 35, 677;

Kahan, K., (1989). Causation and Incentives to Take Care Under Negligence Rule, 18 Journal of Legal Studies, 427;

Kang, J., et al., (2011). Implicit bias in the courtroom. 59 UCLA L. Rev., 1124.

Kang, J., (2014). Rethinking Intent and Impact: Some Behavioral Realism About Equal Protection, 66(3) Alabama Law Review, 627;

Kaplow, L., (1994). The Value of Accuracy in Adjudication: An Economic Analysis. 23(1) The Journal of Legal Studies, 345;

Kaplow, L., (2015). Information and the Aim of Adjudication: Truth or Consequences. 67 Stanford Law Review, 1303;

Kaplow, L., and Shavell, S., (1996). Accuracy in the Assessment of Damages. The Journal of Law and Economics, 39(1), 191;

Kaplow L. and Shavell S., (2002). Economic Analysis of Law, in Handbook of Public Economics (A.J Auerbach and M. Feldstein Eds.), Vol. 3, Elsevier Science B.V., 1669;

Kaplow, L., and Shavell, S., (2003). Fairness Versus Welfare: Notes on the Pareto Principles, Preferences, and Distributive Justice. 32 Journal of Legal Studies 331. Legal Stud., 32, 331;

Karapanou, V., Visscher L. T., (2010). Towards a Better Assessment of Pain and Suffering Damages, 1 Journal of European Tort Law, 48;

Cooper-Stephenson, K., (1978). Damages for Loss of Working Capacity for Women, 43 Sask Law Review, 7;

Kaye J. S., and Lippman J., (2006). Action Plan for the Justice Courts, State of New York Unified Court System;

Kassin, S. M., and Sukel, H., (1997). Coerced confessions and the jury: An experimental test of the" harmless error" rule. Law and Human Behavior, 21(1), 27;

Kelley, H. H., (1973). The Process of Causal Attribution, 28(2) American Psychologist 107;

Kerkmeester H. and L. Visscher L., (2003) Learned Hand in Europe: a Study in the Comparative Law and Economics of Negligence, German Working Papers in Law and Economics, Vol. (6);

Kniesner, T. J., Viscusi, W. K., and Ziliak, J. P., (2014). Willingness to accept Accept Eequals Wwillingness to Ppay for Llabor Mmarket Eestimates of the Vvalue of a Sstatistical Llife. 48(3) Journal of Risk and Uncertainty, 48(3), 187;

Knetsch, J. L., (2015). The Ccuriously Ccontinuing Saga of Choosing the Measure of Welfare Cchanges. 6(1) Journal of Benefit-Cost Analysis, 6(01), 217;

Koppel, S., and Fondacaro, M. R., (2016). The Retribution Heuristic. The Routledge Handbook of Criminal Justice Ethics, 191;

Korobkin, R. B., and Ulen, T. S., (2000). 88(4) Law and Behavioral Science: Removing the Rationality Assumption from Law and Economics. California Law Review, 1051;

Kraus, M. W., and Keltner, D., (2013). Social Cclass Rrank, Eessentialism, and Ppunitive Jjudgment. 105(2) Journal of Personality and Social Psychology, 105(2), 247;

Krueger, J. I., and Funder, D. C., (2004). Social psychology: A field in search of a center. 27(3) Behavioral and Brain Sciences, 361;

Kubota, J. T., Banaji M. R., Phelps E. A., (2012). The Neuroscience of Race. 15(7) Nature Neurosci, 940;

Kunda, Z. (1990). The Case for Motivated Reasoning, 108(3) Psychological Bulletin, 480;

Lamb, S. R., (1996). Toward Gender– Neutral Data for Adjudicating Lost Future Earning Damages: An Evidentiary Perspective, 72 Chicago-Kent Law Review, 299;

Landes, W. (1971). An Economic Analysis of the Courts, 14 Journal of Law and Economics 61;

Lando, H., (2006). Does Wrongful Conviction Lower Deterrence? 35(2) The Journal of Legal Studies 327;

Landsman, S., and Rakos, R. F., (1994). A Preliminary Inquiry Into the Effect of Potentially Biasing Information on Judges and Jurors in Civil Litigation. 12(2) Behavioral Sciences & the Law, 113;

Langevoort, D., (1998). Behavioral Theories of Judgment and Decision Making in Legal Scholarship: A Literature Review, 51 Vand. L. Rev. 1499;

Leidner, B., and Castano E., (2012). Morality Shifting in the Context of Intergroup Violence, 42(1) European Journal of Social Psychology 82;

Lester, J. P., et al., (2001). Environmental injustice in the United States, Boulder, CO: Westview Press;

Levinson, J. D., (2007). Forgotten Racial Equality: Implicit Bias, Decisionmaking, and Misremembering, 57 Duke Law Journal, 345;

Levinson, J. D., and Peng, K., (2004). Different Torts for Different Cohorts: A Cultural Psychological Critique of Tort Law's Actual Cause and Foreseeability Inquiries, 13(2) Southern California Interdisciplinary Law Journal, 195;

Mathur, V. A., et al., (2014). Racial Bias in Pain Perception and Response: Experimental Examination of Automatic and Deliberate Processes, 15(5) The Journal of Pain, 476;

McAdams R., and Ulen T., (2009). Criminal Behavioral Law and Economics. In: N. Garoupa (eds.) Criminal Law and Economics, Edward Elgar, Cheltenham, 403;

Juricial Study Board, (2010). Colin and Great Britain Judicial Studies Board. Guidelines for the Assessment of General Damages in Personal Injury Cases. Oxford University Press;

Ministero della Salute, (2015). Piano d'Azione Salute per e con le Comunità Rom, Sinti e Caminanti;

Miron A. M., et al., (2010). Motivated Shifting of Justice Standards, 20(10) Personality Social Psychology Bullettin, 1;

Mitchell, T. L., et al., (2005). Racial Bias in Mock Juror Decision-making: a Meta-analytic Review of Defendant Treatment, 29 Law and Human Behavior, 627;

Mitchell, G., and Tetlock, P., E., (2006). Antidiscrimination Law and the Perils of Mindreading, 67 Ohio State Law Journal, 1023;

Mitchell, G., and Tetlock, P., (2017). Popularity as a Poor Proxy for Utility. In Psychological Science Under Scrutiny: Recent Challenges and Proposed Solutions, 164;

Mohai P., (2009). Environmental Justice, 34 Annual Review of Environment and Resources, 405;

Mornet B., (2015). L'Indemnisation des Préjudices en Cas de Blessures ou de Décès;

Morris, M. W., and Larrick, R. P., (1995). When One Cause Casts Doubt on Another: A Normative Analysis of Discounting in Causal Attribution. 102(2) Psychological Review, 331;

Newheiser, A. K., et al., (2012). Why Do We Punish Groups? High Entitativity Promotes Moral Suspicion.48(4) Journal of Experimental Social Psychology, 48(4), 931;

Nosek B. A., et al., (2007). Pervasiveness and Correlates of Implicit Attitudes and Stereotypes, 18 European Review of Social Psychology, 36;

OECD-European Union, (2013). The Missing Entrepreneurs: Policies for Inclusive Entrepreneurship in Europe, OECD Publishing;

Oswald, F. L., et al., (2013). Predicting Ethnic and Racial Discrimination: A Meta-Analysis of IAT Criterion Studies, 105(2) Journal of Personality and Social Psychology, 178;

Papillon, K., (2013). The Court's Brain: Neuroscience and Judicial Decision Making in Criminal Sentencing, 49 Court Review, 48;

Payne, B. K., and Gawronski, B., (2012). A History of Implicit Social Cognition: Where Is It Coming From? Where Is It Now? Where Is It Going?, in Handbook of Implicit Social Cognition: Measurement, Theory, and Applications, (B.K. Payne and B. Gawronski Eds.), Guilford Press;

Pellow, D. N., (2002). Garbage wars: The struggle for environmental justice in Chicago, MIT Press;

Pettigrew, T. F., (1979). The Ultimate Attribution Error: Extending Allport's Cognitive Analysis of Prejudice. 5(4) Personality and Social Psychology Bulletin, 461;

Png, I. P., (1986). Optimal Subsidies and Damages in the Presence of Judicial Error. 6(1) International Review of Law and Economics, 101;

Porat, A., (2011). Misalignments in Tort Law, 121 YALE L.aw Journal, 82;

Posner, R. A., (1989). An Economic Analysis of Sex Discrimination Laws. 56(4) The University of Chicago Law Review, 1317;

Posner, R. A., (1998). Rational Choice, Behavioral Economics, and the Law. 50 Stanford Law Review, 1551;

Posner, R. A., (1999). An Economic Approach to the Law of Evidence. Stanford Law Review, 1485;

Posner, R. A., (2011). Economic Analysis of Law, 8th ed., 2011;

Pulido, L., (2000). Rethinking Environmental Racism: White Privilege and Urban Development in Southern California. 90(1) Annals of the Association of American Geographers, 12;

Rachlinski, J. J., et al., (2009). Does Unconscious Racial Bias Affect Trial Judges? 84(3) Notre Dame Law Rev 84(3), 1195;

Rachlinski, J. J., (2011). The Psychological Foundations of Behavioral Law and Economics. 201(5) University of Illinois Law Review, 1675;

Rachlinski, J. J., Guthrie, C., and Wistrich, A. J., (2011). Probable Cause, Probability, and Hindsight. 8(1) Journal of Empirical Legal Studies, 72;

Rachlinski J. J. et al., (2015). Can Judges Make Reliable Numeric Judgments: Distorted Damages and Skewed Sentences, 90 Indiana Law Journal, 7726;

Ratcliff J. J. et al., (2010). The Hidden Consequences of Racial Salience in Videotaped Interrogations and Confessions, 16(2) Psychol Public Policy Law, 200;

Reilly v. United States, 665 F. Supp. 976, 997 (D.R.I. 1987);

Reeder, G. D., (1982). Let's Give the Fundamental Attribution Error Another Chance, 43(2) Journal of Personality and Social Psychology, 341;

Richerson, J. A., and Shelton, J. N., (2005). Brief Report: Thin Slices of Racial Bias, 29(1) Journal of Nonverbal Behavior, 75;

Ross, L., (1977). The Intuitive Psychologist and His Shortcomings: Distortions in the Attribution Process. 10 Advances in Experimental Social Psychology, 173;

Ross, L., and Shestowsky, D., (2002). Contemporary Psychology's Challenges to Legal Theory and Practice. 97 Northwestern University Law Revieww. UL Rev, 97, 1081;

Rubin, M., Hewstone, M., and Voci, A., (2001). Stretching the Bboundaries: Strategic Pperceptions of Iintragroup Vvariability. 31(4) European Journal of Social Psychology, 31(4), 413;

Ravenell, J., and Ogedegbe, G., (2014). Unconscious Bias and Real-World Hypertension Outcomes: Advancing Disparities Research, 29(7) JGIM, 973;

Romano, A., (2016). God's Dice: The Law in a Probalistic World, 41(1) University of Dayton Law Review, 57;

Rubin, M., and Badea, C., (2012). They're All the Same!... but for Several Different Reasons: A Review of the Multicausal Nature of Perceived Group Variability. 21(6) Current Directions in Psychological Science, 21(6), 367;

Rumiati, R., (2014). Errori Cognitivi Sistematici di Rilevanza Forense nel Giudizio Umano;

Sabin, G. A., (2008). Physician Implicit Attitudes and Stereotypes About Race and Quality of Medical Care, 46(7) Medical Care, 678;

Sabin, J. A., et al., (2009). Physicians' Implicit and Explicit Attitudes About Race by MD Race, Ethnicity, and Gender, 20(3) Journal of Health Care for the Poor and the Underserved, 896;

Sabin, J. A., and Greenwald A. G., (2012). The Influence of Implicit Bias on Treatment Recommendations for 4 Common Pediatric Conditions: Pain, Urinary Tract Infection, Attention Deficit Hyperactivity Disorder, and Asthma, 102(5) American Journal of Public Health, 988;

Sandefur, R. L., (2008). Access to civil justice and race, class, and gender inequality. 34 Annual Review of Sociology, 340;

Shavers, V. L., et al., (2012). Research on Race/Ethnicity and Health Care Discrimination: Where We Are and Where We Need to Go, 102(5) American Journal of Public Health, 930;

Sommers, S. R., and Ellsworth, P.C., (2009). "Race Salience" in Juror Decision-Making: Misconceptions, Clarifications, and Unanswered Questions, (2009) 27(4) Behavioral Sciences & the Law, 599;

Stanley, D. A., et al., (2011). Implicit Race Attitudes Predict Trustworthiness Judgment and Economic Trust Decisions, 108(19) PNAS, 7710;

Sue, D. W., (2008). Racial Microaggressions in the Life Experience of Black Americans, 39(3) Professional Psychology - Research & Practice, 329;

Sue, D. W., (2010). Microaggressions in Everyday Life: Race, Gender, and Sexual Orientation, Wiley & Sons;

Sue, D. W., et al., (2007). Racial Microaggressions in Everyday Life Implications for Clinical Practice, 62(4) American Psychologist, 272;

Sugarman, S. D., (1985). Doing Away with Tort Law. 73(3) California Law Review, 555;

Posner, R. A., (2010). How Judges Think. Harvard University Press;

Prentice, R. A., (2012). Behavioral Economics Applied: Loss Causation. 44 Loyiala University Chicago Law Journal, 1509;

Quintano, C., et al., (2013). A Cross-Country Analysis of Gender Pay Gap and Segregation. 2 Italian Journal of Applied Statistics, 2, 2;

Shavell, S., (1980). Strict Liability Versus Negligence. 9(1) The Journal of Legal Studies, 1;

Shavell, S., (2009). Economic Analysis of Accident Law. Harvard University Press;

Sheldon, J., and Murray, P., (2003). Rethinking the Rules of Evidentiary Admissibility in Non-Jury Trials, 86 Judicature, 231;

Shoda, T. M., (2014). Having Explicit-Implicit Evaluation Discrepancies Triggers Race-Based Motivated Reasoning, 32(2) Social Cognition, 190;

Shoda, T. M., et al., (2014). Implicit Consistency Processes in Social Cognition: Explicit-Implicit Discrepancies Across Systems of Evaluation, 8(3) Social and Personality Psychology Compass, 135;

Singer, R. B., (2005). How to prepare Prepare a Llife Eexpectancy Rreport for an Aattorney in a Tort Case. J. Insurance Medicine, 37 Journal of Insurance medicine, 37;

Silvera, D. H., et al., (2000). The Association between Implicit Theories of Personality and the Attribution Process, 41 The Scandinavian Journal of Psychology, 107;

Sood, A. M., (2013). Motivated Cognition in Legal Judgments – An Analytic Review, 9 Annual Review Law Social Science, 307;

Stein, A., (2005). Foundations of Evidence Law, Oxford University Press, 141;

Stein, A., (2015). The New Doctrinalism: Implications for Evidence Theory, 51(6) University of Pennsylvania Law Review, 163;

Snyder, M. L., and Jones, E. E., (1974). Attitude Attribution when Behavior is Constrained. 10 Journal of Experimental Social Psychology, 10, 585;

Tam K., et al., (2013). Belief about Immutability of Moral Characters and Punitiveness Toward Criminal Offenders, 43 Journal of Applied Social Psychology, 608;

Tarrant, M., et al., (2012). Social Identity and Perceptions of Torture: It's Moral When We Do It, 48(2) Journal of Experimental Social Psychology, 513;

Taruffo, M., (2012). La Prova nel Processo Civile, 424;

Tetlock, P. E., (1985). Accountability: A Social Check of the Fundamental Attribution Error, 48(3) Social Psychology Quarterly, 227;

Teichman, D., and Zamir, E., (2014). Judicial Decisionmaking: A Behavioral Perspective. The Oxford Handbook of Behavioral Economics and the Law. Zamir, E., & Teichman, D. (Eds.) Oxford University Press;

The Law Commission Report (1999). No 257 Damages for Non-Pecuniary Loss;

Tobler, C., (2011). Case C-236/09, Association Belge des Consommateurs Test-Achats ASBL, Yann van Vurgt, Charles Basselier v. Conseil des ministres. 48 Common Market Law Reviewl 2041;

Tor, A., (2008). The Methodology of the Behavioral Analysis of Law. 4 Haifa Law Review, 239;

Tunçel, T., and Hammitt, J. K., (2014). A new New Meta-analysis on the WTP/WTA Disparity. 68(1) Journal of Environmental Economics and Management, 68(1), 175;

Tversky, A., and Kahneman, D. (1974). Judgment under Uncertainty: Heuristics and Biases. , 185(4157) Science , 1124;

U.S. Gov't Accountability Office, (1990). GAO GGD-90-557, Death Penalty Sentencing: Research Indicates Pattern of Racial Disparities, 5;

United States v. Bedonie, 317 F.Supp.2d at 1319 (2004);

United States v. Serawop, 505 F.3d 1112, at 1126 (10th Cir. 2007);

United States v. Bedonie, 317 F.Supp.2d at 1319 (2004);

Varnum, M. E., Na, J., Murata, A., and Kitayama, S., (2012). Social Class Differences in N400 Indicate Differences in Spontaneous Trait Inference. 141(3) Journal of Experimental Psychology: General, 518;

Vars, F. E., (2014). Behavioural Economics and Evidence Law, The Oxford handbook of behavioral economics and the law. Zamir, E., & Teichman, D. (Eds.) Oxford University Press. 703;

van Velthoven, B. C. J., (2009). Empirics of Tort, In Tort Law and Economics, Ed. Michael Faure, 2nd Edition, Edward Elgar, 453;

Vincent, J., and Guinchard, S., (2003). Procédure Civile Dalloz 768;

Vladescu, E., (2006). The Assimilation of Immigrant Groups in France–Myth or Reality?. 5(39) Jean Monnet/Robert Schuman Paper Series, 5(39), 1;

Voci, A., (2000). Perceived Group Variability and the Salience of Personal and Social Identity, 11(1) European Review of Social Psychology, 11(1), 177;

Wallace D. B., and Kassin, S. M., (2012). Harmless Error Analysis: How Do Judges Respond to Confession Errors?, 36(2) Law and Human Behavior, 155;

Wistrich, A. J., Guthrie, C. and Rachlinski, J. J., (2005). Can Judges Ignore Inadmissible Information? The Difficulty of Deliberately Disregarding. 153(4) University of Pennsylvania Law Review 1251;

Wistrich, A. J., Rachlinski, J. J., and Guthrie, C., (2014). Heart Versus Head: Do Judges Follow the Law of Follow their Feelings. 93 Texas Law Review, 85;

Wriggins, J. B., (2007). Damages in Tort Litigation: Thoughts on Race and Remedies, 1865-2007. 27(1) Review of Litigation, 37;

Xu X. et al., (2009). Do You Feel My Pain? Racial Group Membership Modulates Empathic Neural Responses, 29 Neuroscience, 8525;

Zimbardo, P. G., (2007). Lucifer Effect. Blackwell Publishing Ltd;

Zimbardo, P. G., (2004). A Situationist Perspective on the Psychology of Evil: Understanding How Good People Are Transformed into Perpetrators. The Social Psychology of Good and Evil, 21;

The manufacturer's authorised representative in the EU is Springer Nature Customer Service Centre GmbH, Europaplatz 3, 69115 Heidelberg, Germany. If you have any concerns regarding our products, please contact ProductSafety@springernature.com

Printed and bound by CPI Group (UK) Ltd, Croydon, CR0 4YY
28/09/2026
02224076-0007